green tea

living

green tea

living

A Japan-Inspired
Guide to Eco-friendly
Habits, Health, and Happiness

Toshimi A. Kayaki
with illustrations by Miyuki Matsuo

Stone Bridge Press • Berkeley, California

Published by
Stone Bridge Press
P.O. Box 8208
Berkeley, CA 94707
510-524-8732 • sbp@stonebridge.com • www.stonebridge.com

Text © 2010 Toshimi A. Kayaki.

Printed in the United States of America.

2012 2011 2010 2009   10 9 8 7 6 5 4 3 2 1

Library of Congress Cataloging-in-Publication data avaialble upon request.

ISBN 978-1-933330-84-6

Contents

introduction

GREEN TEA DREAMS

"If you have a dream, go after it. You can and will have your American dream."

Do you believe that?

Here is the story of the long, long road I traveled to realize my American dream.

My American husband, Sam, and I moved back to the U.S. from Japan with two little sons in 1989. Sam had lived in Japan for eleven years, and we had been married for the last eight of those. After we moved to California, he went back to graduate school.

We faced many hardships raising the kids and paying the bills.

"After he gets his Master's Degree, I will have a nice, big American house," I dreamed.

But somehow Sam fell into poor health after graduate school. He had heart problems, skin cancer, two hip replacements, leukemia, pneumonia, and serious backaches. He had to be hospitalized seven times.

Our lives turned around and went the wrong way. Everything got harder. His illnesses kept on and on, each one worse than the one before.

Eventually, he ended up in an ICU in critical condition. His health was turbulent.

Of course, each sickness affected the finances and emotions of the whole family.

On top of Sam's faltering health, renting houses was full of uncertainty and aggravation. We had bad luck with our landlords. We had to move three times in two years because each house we were renting went up for sale. "Don't worry. I won't be ready to sell for years," each of the landlords had said to us in almost the exact same words. We felt so foolish for trusting in each of them.

Having little kids and moving so often was driving us crazy.

Not only that, we were eating all the wrong foods—too many sweets, sodas, and starchy stuff. Each of us gained weight. The boys and I got chubby, and Sam got fat.

A Vision of the Future

No more sickness! No more renting houses! No more fat! No more poor!

Reality was rough, but I kept holding on to a vision of happiness and wealth for the future.

The question was—how?

What could I do?

When could I purchase a house?

The first thing we had to do was begin to save money. We had to change our lifestyle.

I didn't want to have to be stingy in order to save because I wanted us to have a good life in California—to eat healthful meals, to be physically fit, and to go out and have fun with our kids. I needed to change in reasonable and subtle ways.

Since our kids were small, we went on picnics or to the beach or to the mountains and forests. We taught our boys the benevolence of nature, the love of the land.

I made *bento* lunch boxes and wrapped them up in a *furo-shiki*, a kind of "eco-cloth." (It can be used as a mat, too.)

The boys played and ran over hills and fields, and through the streams and surf. These simple pleasures made for valuable family time.

It was during our family outings that I started to think about my grandmother in Japan.

She knew how to save money, maintain good health, give to and receive from nature, and lead an eco-friendly life.

What was traditional and old from Japan would be new again in our American family.

Green Tea Living!

Grandma died when she was ninety-four years old, just a couple of years before we moved to California. We were living with her in her big house until she passed away. She was energetic, open-minded, and sharp. She could even read an English children's book to my son, and, for the most part, she was healthy up until the last day of her life, when her heart just stopped.

I started to do things Grandma's Way little by little. I cut the utility bill, the water bill, food, gas, cleaning products, dry cleaning, cosmetics, and more and more to save up to $300 monthly.

The traditional Japanese ways were a good match for

keeping us out of debt and in better health. Our income was not much, but we tried to manage as best we could and save money, too. Eleven years later, we were finally able to buy a house on a hill overlooking San Francisco Bay.

We changed a lot of things about our diet—we went from coffee to green tea, bread to brown rice, milk to soymilk, steak to tofu, French Fries to *edamame*, and candy and sweets to fruit. We ate more fish than meat. All of us slimmed down.

Sam's improved health included lower cholesterol and normal blood pressure. He finished graduate school and his internship and is now a licensed psychotherapist in private practice in Millbrae near San Francisco.

My son Nick moved to Japan after he graduated from college and started work at an IT company. He now works 12 hours a day, just like the Japanese. He has become the youngest manager at his company at the age of twenty-six. He sticks to the traditional Japanese diet, and he is very healthy and energetic.

My son Julian is a young adult and a professional model and personal trainer here in California. He is very strict about what he eats and drinks. He has green tea in the morning and almost never drinks coffee. He eats brown rice instead of white, and he gets a healthy workout at the fitness club every day.

As for me, I love living here in California. I've adapted to the American way of life, yet I continue many of the traditions I learned growing up in Japan. I drink at least five cups of green tea a day. I hang the laundry out to dry. I walk instead of drive as much as possible.

I kept up with my writing for Japanese publications, but I had always wanted to write a book in English. So, this book is another realization of my Green Tea Dream. All things added together, my American Dream has pretty much come true.

Following Grandma's Way, I learned that Green Tea Living can be for anyone who wants to save money, be healthy, happy, and eco-friendly as well.

Green Tea Living can take you on a new journey toward feeling good and living within your means.

Acknowledgments

After I turned forty, I realized I was attending more funerals than weddings or other celebrations. Clearly, my life was moving through time toward new purpose. New chapters had to be written.

I kept asking myself what I wanted to do for the rest of my life. One day I started a search on the Internet to see if any of the books I had written in Japanese would show up. I found that even here in America, and in a few other countries, several of my books were available at universities and public libraries.

My heart leapt with joy!

What satisfaction as an author! I had dreamt of people around the world reading my stories. I wanted to share more, so I decided I would write a book in English, and now I have done it.

I thank my husband, Sam Anram, for bringing me to America. He has helped me open up my heart and mind to a world of possibilities. His devotion and support have guided me every day.

Thanks also to my sons, Nick and Julian, who encouraged me to stick to my writing even through the toughest times.

Special thanks to my Grandmother Ryu, my mother Kurako,

and my sister Junko Kayaki, whose experience and knowledge of the Japanese traditions inspired me to share our ways with the readers.

I thank Toky o-based artist Miyuki Matsuo for her delightful Japanese-style drawings, which give the book its unique style of presentation.

I also thank Vernon Johnson, my life coach, who made it clear to me to never give up.

Thanks to my friends Michiko Ibuka and Hiroko Falkenstein for supporting me in my writing during this long journey.

I very much appreciate my publisher, Peter Goodman, who gave me the opportunity to publish this book. He was always quick to respond to me, even late at night or early in the morning. Every little push and comment kept me on track to completion.

TAK

1

a green tea life

INTRODUCTION

My husband lay feverish and weak from bacterial pneumonia in a hospital ICU here in California several years ago.

In came the food server with his dinner. Along with roast chicken, mashed potatoes, and Jell-O, was coffee on the tray. I was momentarily immobile with astonishment.

"Can an almost dying person eat this food and drink coffee?" I thought.

"Are they trying to kill him?"

"Don't they know how coffee can upset his stomach and over-stimulate his heart?"

"Do Americans have entirely different internal organs?"

After the initial shock subsided, I contemplated, "What would the Japanese serve a sick person to drink?"

Green tea!

After that, I started to research the benefits of green tea.

According to medical studies done by Dr. Andrew Weil, clinical professor of Internal Medicine at the University of Arizona and a world-renowned integrative medicine expert, there's a specific antioxidant in green tea, known as EGCG, that shows "impressive activity against many kinds of cancer, while appearing to protect the heart and arteries from oxidative damage."

A new Japanese scientific study (October 2009) says that green tea can fight againshe H1N1 flu. Tokushima Bunri University research reports that it is the catechins from the green tea that can fight against the virus.

Green tea affects not only the body. In the section "Drinking green tea for relaxation," below, I mention a study that shows how green tea helps reduce stress. It is easy for me to believe the reports of science because when I was young, Grandma told me having green tea was not only for enjoying the taste. It's a natural medicine. It can help body and mind to keep a healthy balance.

I believe green tea always helped me to get better when I was sick. When I am sad, angry, anxious, or feeling physically ill with an upset stomach, diarrhea, or fatigue, I have to have my green tea. Green tea has become a part of my life.

Green tea is, as we say in Japanese, *yasashii*. That means gentle and mild. It's like soft cotton on the skin to me.

Green tea is well known all over the world now for its enjoyable flavor as well as for promoting weight loss and longevity.

But there is so much more to living a vibrant life the way the Japanese do.

GREEN "BEAUTEA"3 HELP FOR AGING

I know a lady who works on her farm all day, every day, but she doesn't look like a farmer. Her skin is smooth, youthful, and moisturized. She has almost no age spots or wrinkles.

With so much sunshine soaking into her skin day after day, why does she still look so young? "It's green tea!" she says.

But this time it's not drinking green tea. She actually packs it on her face, and this is how you can do it too:

1. Grind up used green tea leaves into a fine, almost powdery substance.
2. Mix the green substance with water and flour until it thickens into a paste.
3. Wash your face and apply the pack for 10 minutes.
4. Rinse it off with water; then put on your favorite lotion.

5. . . . or instead of paste, just put tea bags on your face

I've tried this, and it's working. My skin is getting smoother and my age spots are fading away. Now I don't need to hide my skin under a dark foundation.

It's inexpensive, it's cosmopolitan, and it's eco-friendly, too!

GREEN TEA TO HELP MAINTAIN
HEALTHY BODY WEIGHT

Drinking green tea is getting so popular, you can order it in coffee shops, too—here in California, at least.

Have you seen all the ads for weight loss by drinking green tea? Are they telling the truth?

My whole life I have believed that green tea is good for my health. When I drink it, I feel refreshed. It calms the spirit and eases the mind. But I never thought it had anything to do with losing weight.

When I was watching "The Oprah Winfrey Show," I heard for the first time that people drink green tea to shed pounds. Japanese researchers claim that drinking five cups of green tea a day can burn 70 to 80 extra calories. Dr Nicholas Perricone, a self-proclaimed anti-aging specialist, appeared on "Oprah" that day and told her viewers they can lose 10 pounds in six weeks drinking green tea instead of coffee.

After this show, green tea became a hot media topic. But I still wasn't clear on why it helps weight loss, so I researched the Japanese reports. And they say it does help if you drink it *before* eating meals. Green tea contains catechins, which help make a film on the lining of the stomach. This coating prevents the intake of extra calories and stimulates the burning of more! It keeps you regular, too.

If you want to drink green tea for losing weight, remember to have a cup just before you eat. It works.

GREEN TEA FERTILIZER

After drinking green tea, you can use the leftover leaves for fertilizing your flowers or vegetable garden.

Mix the green tea leaves into the dirt for gardening.

The leaves will ferment and make the soil rich.

In case you've been using other kinds of raw garbage to make compost, consider this: much of it contains salt because

it has been processed or cooked. Green tea leaves, however, are 100% natural, so they enrich the soil without polluting it with sodium chloride.

You can put the green tea leaves in planters and flowerpots, too.

Just put the leaves on top of the soil around the plant or flower, then water. The tea leaves will hold moisture into the dirt. After my skin pack, I always put the leaves into my potted plants.

How wonderful—a terrific triple bonus! This is really green living.

GREEN TEA CAVITY PROTECTION

Here is an interesting report about cavities and green tea.

Japanese elementary school kids have too many cavities in their teeth. One elementary school in Kyoto had its young students participate in an experiment using green tea for gargling every day after lunch. Three years later, there was a 50% decrease in the number of cavities among those children.

According to a study by the Tokyo Medical and Dental School, the fluorine in green tea actually does make strong teeth. Catechins protect teeth from plaque. Tannins kill bacteria inside the mouth.

After a meal, try gargling with green tea. You don't have to do it three times a day. Even just once a day should be enough.

It will help. Don't you think it would be better than putting liquid chemicals in your mouth?

Green tea is safe and economical.

DRINKING GREEN TEA FOR RELAXATION

When I am nervous or worried, my body and mind call for green tea. After having a cup or two, I can relax. I don't know why it helps; I just follow Grandma's way.

She always told me to drink green tea if I was tense. I took it for granted that she knew what she was talking about. Current medical reports seem to confirm that she was right.

According to a study at the Nagoya University Department of Psychology in 2007, L-theanine is an amino acid in green tea leaves known to block the binding of L-glutamic acid to glutamate receptors in the brain.

Because the characteristics of L-theanine suggest that it may influence psychological and physiological states under stress, it was suggested that the oral intake of L-theanine could have stress-reducing effects by inhibiting stimulation of cortical neurons.

My friend in France said that even there, drinking green tea is a chic and health-conscious thing to do. Her French friends realize that green tea has caffeine but it doesn't make them feel irritated or jittery. Rather, they say, it has the opposite effect—it soothes and relaxes. However, it seems to brighten mind and spirit. L-theanine must do the trick!

Now I can tell my friends about the secret of green tea.

GREEN TEA BATHS FOR CLEAN, SMOOTH SKIN

Five years ago, I heard from my friend about green tea bathing.

I was incredulous. Put green tea in the bathwater? Then my friend rolled up her sleeves and pulled up her pant legs and showed me her skin. It was silky smooth. She told me she had had dry, flaky skin for many years and tried many remedies, but the green tea bathing had cleaned and smoothed her skin.

I found out that green tea has a lot of vitamins—five times more than lemon, in fact. The catechins in green tea kill surface bacteria, and help to clear up damaged skin.

A German study found that an extract of green tea mixed

with filtered hot water applied to the skin three times a day for 10 minutes helped repair skin damaged by radiation therapy in sixteen to twenty-two days.

Here's how to make a Green Tea Bath:

1. Put 1 ounce (30 g) of green tea in a small cotton bag.
2. Tie the bag and put it in boiling water for 15 minutes.
3. Pour the hot green tea water into your bath and relax.

BANISH SMELLY FISH ODORS WITH GREEN TEA

I love fish for meals.

In Japan, I ate so many different kinds of fish.

I enjoyed baked, fried, sautéed, marinated, boiled, and raw fish (*sashimi*). I can prepare fish dozens of ways.

One thing that disappoints me in America is that I can't find very many different kinds of fish at the supermarket.

Not only that, I had trouble at home each time I cooked fish. The whole house smelled of fish.

My boys didn't like it, especially when their friends came

over. They didn't want to have smelly fish even the day before their buddies were supposed to come to play or have a sleepover. They said the fish smell stayed overnight.

I talked about this with my mother. She told me Grandma usually used green tea to take away the fish smell. She always put tea leaves in hot water in the empty baking pan and left it in the oven after taking out the cooked fish. She ate fish every day, but her house never smelled of it.

I fry fish on the stovetop because it's easy. It only takes a few minutes, and then I sprinkle used green tea leaves into the frying pan, add a little water, turn off the gas, and leave the pan on the still-warm burner. The fishy smell vanishes right away. Amazing!

POWER CLEANING WITH GREEN TEA LEAVES

Green tea is not just good for your health.

Japanese have been using it for cleaning and deodorizing for centuries.

After drinking green tea, don't discard the wet tea leaves right away. Put them in your hand and squeeze to take out most of the water.

Don't take out all of the water; you'll need some moisture because you're going to clean with it.

Wet tea leaves are perfect for dusting the floor—wood, tile, tatami mats, concrete, or almost any surface where there is dust.

It's especially good for getting dust and hair out of corners or little nooks and crannies. The dirt particles cling to the wet tea leaves. The trick is to take a broom and sweep the leaves back and forth in small strokes until you can see that the dust and hair has been lifted up. Then just sweep everything into the dustpan.

Tea contains catechin, which kills bacteria and odors. I recommend it for cleaning the bathroom floor. When you are done, you can smell the green tea fragrance. How refreshing!

Forget spending extra money on harsh, toxic chemical floor cleaners.

Green tea cleaning is safe for babies and small kids who touch the floor all the time.

It does the eco-friendly job right.

GREEN TEA FOR A HEALTHY HEART AND LOWER BLOOD PRESSURE

A recent study (*Time* 2008) shows evidence that green tea, which is more popular in Eastern culture, has cardiovascular benefits. According to Dr. Nikolaos Alexopoulos of Athens Medical School in Greece, green tea can protect the heart arteries by keeping them flexible and relaxed and thus better able to withstand the ups and downs of constant changes in blood pressure.

People who drank green tea showed greater dilation of their heart arteries on ultrasound 30 minutes after drinking it compared to those drinking either diluted caffeine or hot water.

Scientists speculate green tea works on the lining of blood vessels.

When doctors measured the green tea drinkers' arteries two weeks after daily consumption of the beverage, they found that their blood vessels were more dilated than they had been at the beginning of the study. They recommend having a bit less than ¼ ounce (6 g) of green tea daily, which amounts to 3 to 4 cups a day.

I have at least five cups a day, and so far I have normal blood pressure and no heart disease.

HAVE A GREEN TEA MORNING

Isn't it hard to wake up alert and be ready to go in the morning?

After you wake up, your brain may still be dull. Your body doesn't want to get up out of the chair at the breakfast table. The inside of your mouth feels sticky, and your breath smells bad.

If you always think you need a cup of coffee to wake you up, how about trying a cup of green tea next time? There are three reasons I recommend it.

1. It refreshes the mouth: Green tea has tannin, which takes away the stickiness and bad

smells from your mouth. The tannin kills bacteria, too.

2. It wakes up your brain: Green tea has caffeine and helps stimulate your mind.
3. It's got vitamins: Coffee and English tea don't have Vitamin C, but green tea does; there are 280 mg of Vitamin C in 100 g of green tea leaves.

So if you have a cup of green tea, you don't need coffee, mouthwash, or orange juice. You get everything you need all in one warm, natural drink. Among the many kinds of green tea, Sen-Cha may be the best choice for the early hours of your day, since it has more caffeine than other types of green tea; in other words, it is better at waking your system and getting you going for the new day.

HOW TO MAKE DELICIOUS GREEN TEA

In a study of more than 40,500 Japanese men and women, those who drank the most cups of green tea every day had the lowest risk of dying from heart disease and stroke.

So would you like to try green tea today?

You really need only one or two cups of green tea every day to start doing your heart some good—but you need to brew it yourself. Ready-made teas don't offer the same health benefits. "Once water is added to tea leaves, their catechins degrade within a few days," says Jeffrey Blumberg, Ph.D., a professor of nutrition science and policy at Tufts University.

If you drink other kinds of English teas, adding milk may eliminate tea's protective effects on the cardiovascular system, so stick to just lemon or honey. The best way is to not add anything. Better yet, just have green tea.

Here is how to make green tea:

1. Pour hot water into each cup that you will serve. This helps to cool down the boiling water. The best temperature for tea is 158°–176°F (70°–80°C).
2. Put the tea leaves into the teapot. Use about 2 tablespoons (7 g) of tea for five people.
3. Transfer the hot water from the cups into the teapot.
4. Wait 30 seconds.
5. Fill up each cup evenly, little by little, until the pot is empty. Pour back and forth between the cups to get the same flavor in each one. The tea should not be too strong or too weak.

2

green
tea
cuisine

INTRODUCTION

Each country has different traditional foods.

I have heard that when soy sauce first came to America, people thought it smelled like bug spray. Now, of course, millions of people enjoy it in a variety of dishes.

Many years ago, my husband, I, and our elder son moved into my grandmother's house in Japan. On the first morning, my husband woke early and went to the kitchen to make coffee. He was curious about everything, especially in the kitchen, so he opened cans and containers to see what was inside. Suddenly, I heard him gasping and shouting. "What is this stuff? It looks like a bucket full of crap!"

He has taken the lid off a bucket at the end of the kitchen counter and found a gooey, yellow-color paste. My husband was talking so loudly, Grandma came to see what had happened.

When she saw the bucket was uncovered, she got upset.

"This is very important to me. This paste, called *nukamiso*, is over forty years old! I use it to make pickles, I've been using it since before World War II. If I have pickles and rice, I can survive anything."

Nuka is rice bran, used for pickling (*nukazuke*) the *tsukemono* of Japan.

It contains various antioxidants that impart beneficial effects on human health.

Grandma's *nukazuke* was the pride of her kitchen, but my husband thought it looked like baby poop.

It's obvious that one of the biggest differences between cultures is the food. My husband decided to be openminded about that. Once he started to eat Grandma's pickles, he acquired a taste for them. In fact, he grew to love them.

And now I'm making *nukazuke* here in America.

It is like soy sauce. Once you get used to it, you like it.

Other foods—tofu, *wakame* (seaweed), *konnyaku* (made from the konjac plant—a rubbery, vegan gel), *soba* (buckwheat noodles), and *natto* (fermented soybeans)—are wonderful, and healthy. The good news is that these foods are economical and low-calorie as well as nutritious.

Usually, diet food in America is more expensive, but these foods are cheaper and healthier to eat while helping you to take off the weight.

Good food can pass through borders from country to country.

People learn what they like, what's good and good for them.

I hope you can try some of my favorite foods.

FILL UP 80%

I was watching a TV talk show in Japan. The guest was Dr. Hino-hara.

He is ninety-seven years old and still practicing medicine, writing books and a regular column, and making appearances on TV and radio shows. He conducts seminars not only in Japan but in other countries. He came to San Francisco when he was ninety-five. He is a very busy doctor. He said his schedule is filled up ten years from now.

One of his health secrets is sleep, but not long hours of sleep—only 4 hours a night. He says people misunderstand. "Long life means long living, not sleeping."

"Even with 4 hours of sleep, I am not tired! I want more time!"

He also said when he has a meal, he eats until his stomach feels a little more than half full, and he doesn't get hungry until it's time for the next meal.

(If you concentrate on work, you will forget about being hungry. Life is about doing what you love!) He said for elderly people, eating to about 60% full is best, while most adults need to fill up their stomachs to about 80%.

Hara 8 bunme,isha irazu
Fill your stomach 80%, and then you don't need a doctor.

The Japanese say this all the time. This means before you feel completely full, stop eating and make space for some green tea, and you will finish up full and satisfied with your meal. The food is digested easily, and you won't get an upset stomach.

Some medical researchers wanted to check out this old wisdom, so they performed an experiment with mice. They kept the mice 80% full of food every day. They figured out the mice had more energy than overly fed mice, and they had less chance of getting cancer.

Your body makes many new cells every day and changes them. If you use up energy, the bad cells naturally die (apoptosis). This results in less cancer of the liver, colon, and breasts.

Actually, this traditional way of eating can help you deal with the rising cost of food.

For example, if you paid $10 for meat and vegetables last year, and now you have to pay $12, don't complain! This is a chance to improve your health and slim down. Just keep spending $10 like last year. Of course, you get 20% less food, but that's OK.

Your stomach is 80% full, you'll have more energy, and soon you'll look good, too.

MISO SOUP FOR BREAKFAST

On a busy morning, what is the best breakfast?

Is it a quick bowl of cereal and coffee to wake you up?

Grandma told me if you want to have a healthy way to wake up, have miso soup; it warms up your body quickly and contributes to good health.

What is miso? Miso is a paste made by natural fermentation, which transforms soybeans and grains into a delicious and

versatile staple food.

In the Edo period, people said, "Don't spend money at the doctor's office—spend money for miso." That was written in *The Food Dictionary* published in 1695. People believe miso calms the mind and soothes the stomach. It increases blood circulation, too. Even now, it is used to clean tobacco tar out of pipes. People stock up on miso in case of natural disaster or national crisis. Miso can be kept for years at a time.

Miso's outstanding medicinal qualities have been confirmed in scientific research going back to 1965. Scientists at Japan's National Cancer Research Center found that those who regularly eat miso soup suffer significantly less from some forms of stomach and duodenal cancer, as well as heart disease. In 1972, a researcher from Tohoku University discovered an alkaloid in miso that discharges heavy metal from the body.

So how do you make miso soup on a busy morning?

It is very easy. Put water in a pot and add cut vegetables—anything you like: carrots, green onions, potatoes, cabbage, beans, etc. (You can cut the veggies the night before and put them in the pot with water to save time in the morning. That's what Grandma did). Boil the vegetables until they are soft. Add 1 tablespoon of miso for each person and stir it in. Turn off the stove and remove the pot from the heat.

HIGH-FIBER JAPANESE *KONNYAKU* FOR WEIGHT LOSS

We all know fiber helps us to lose weight, but *konnyaku*, a vegan gel from the konjac plant, works amazingly well to induce weight loss.

The first time I heard about this was when I interviewed a sixteen-year-old gymnast for a magazine article. She told me that before a tournament she would just eat *konnyaku* to keep her weight down and to give her a lot of energy for long hours of hard practice. According to her, *konnyaku* gave her everything she needed in the way of nutrition. Even now, young girls eat *konnyaku* for dieting. It has been an important part of dieting in Japan for many years.

Konnyaku has glucomannan—a good source of dietary fiber—about 13 g of fiber per 100 g of *konnyaku*.

Glucomannan is extremely difficult for humans to digest. Therefore, *konnyaku* usually just goes through your body and cleans out your intestines.

That is why it has been regarded as a good diet food. It fills you up but doesn't add calories.

A new study says that *konnyaku* normalizes the level of cholesterol, prevents high blood pressure, and regulates the level of sugar in the blood. Because of these scientific findings, it is widely perceived as health food.

How to Eat *Konnyaku*

The easy way to eat *konnyaku* is to just slice it thinly and dip it in wasabi and soy sauce or into miso sugar. A traditional way to cook *konnyaku* is to add it to *oden*, a kind of winter soup dish containing lots of fresh seasonal vegetables, radish, fish cake, boiled egg, and soy-flavored *dashi* broth. People like to put it in *sukiyaki*, too.

NATTO

Natto is a most traditional Japanese food. I don't know if people all over the world would like it or not. It has a strong smell and taste and a sticky consistency. It is hard to get used to for non-Japanese people. Many say, "Oh, Yuck! Who can eat this sticky, smelly food?" But many others, like my husband and many of my American friends, have started to enjoy it, and even love it, because *natto* has great health benefits.

 Natto is fermented soybeans, and that's why it has such a pungent odor. Even so, in the late 1990s, *natto* become Japan's most popular food, and now July 10 is the annual Natto Day.

 What is so good about *natto*?

 One medical benefit of *natto* is that it contains *nattokinase* (a serine protease type enzyme), which may decrease the risk of blood clots. Someone who eats *natto* regularly may be less likely to suffer a heart attack, pulmonary embolism, or stroke.

Natto also contains large amounts of Vitamin K, involved in the formation of calcium-binding groups of l proteins. This assists in the formation of bone and in the prevention of osteoporosis. Also, *natto* has very large amounts of Vitamin K2, approximately 870 mcg per 100 g of *natto*. According to recent studies, polyamine suppresses excessive immune reactions, and *natto* contains a much larger amount of it than any other food. Best of all, *natto* is claimed to prevent obesity, possibly due to a low calorie content of approximately 90 calories per 7–8 g of protein in an average serving. Unverified claims include improved digestion and reduced effects of aging.

How to Eat *Natto*

Put the *natto* in a bowl. Just add a little *tare* (a mild kind of soy sauce) or regular soy sauce, if you like, and mix it up with chopsticks until it's really sticky and gooey. Put a little bit at a time on top of rice, and enjoy a delectable mouthful.

SALTY PLUMS WITH EVERYDAY MEALS

The sour, salty plum—*umeboshi*—is a kind of Japanese pickle.

Take a bite of one with rice: your lips will pucker and your mouth will water. They are *really* sour.

Grandma said you don't need that much more to eat if you just have *umeboshi* and rice. This is called *hinomaru-bento* because the rice is white and the plum on top is red, and it looks like the Rising Sun of the Japanese flag when served in a rectangular *bento* box.

This salty plum has a powerful effect on the body. It is said to kill three poisons:

1. It kills harmful bacteria.
2. It takes toxins from the blood.
3. It cleans up retained water in the body.

Salty plums have a lot of citric acid. When the body gets tired, it makes more lactic acid. Eating a salty plum changes this acidity and burns fat; then proteins are free to do their job and you get more energy.

Even nowadays, with so many food choices, Japanese people make an effort to eat *umeboshi* once a day to promote good health.

You get used to the salty and sour taste if you have one or two every day. Once you add *umeboshi* to your diet, you miss its stimulating taste when you don't eat it—and your body will miss it more.

DAIKON FOR A HEALTHY DIET

The daikon is one of the most popular vegetables in Japan.

Daikon means "large root" in Japanese. In America you might call it a white radish, but they sell it by its own name, "daikon," in grocery stores here in California.

The flavor is generally mild—just a little bitter—and it's crunchy and watery like celery.

Daikon is very low in calories. It provides Vitamin C, and the active enzyme myrosinase aids digestion, so it is a good diet vegetable.

How to Eat Daikon

There are many ways to eat this large root.

You can slice it to eat fresh in salads, or you can grate it, as you would a carrot. The grated version is called *daikon oroshi*. Squeeze a little lemon juice and soy sauce in it and eat it with steak or broiled fish. It is really tasty. Japanese steak restaurants use it.

If you've had sashimi, you have already tasted daikon. It's the thin, white, stringy stuff under the raw fish, or it's often boiled with other vegetables in the miso soup that goes along with your sashimi appetizer. But the most

for salad

boil

popular way to prepare daikon is to pickle it. *Takuwan* are daikon pickles.

When you buy a daikon, get a nice long one because there's a different way to use each part of it. At the top, close to the leaves, it is juicy and sweet, so you can use it for salad or *daikon oroshi*. From the center to the bottom it is less juicy. Boil slices from this part with fish or meat, and they will get tender.

ENJOY SEASONAL FOODS

Each of the four seasons in Japan has dynamic changes in weather, the colors of nature, and the harvesting of food. The Japanese very much enjoy these changes, especially the ones related to food, because each season brings its own tasty delights. Nowadays, we can buy frozen seasonal foods at any time of the year, and they can also be grown in greenhouses.

But fresh foods in their own season are high quality and tasty.

Japanese restaurants take a lot of pride in serving fresh seasonal foods prepared in the traditional ways.

Also, seasonal foods are good for your health. They create harmony within the body.

Some warm you up when it's cold, and others cool you off when it's hot.

In the winter there are vegetables like radishes, carrots, brown roots, and so forth.

In the spring, there are green, leafy vegetables. In the

summer there are fruits, like watermelon and strawberries, that contain a lot of water. The body needs these natural waters after perspiring on steamy summer days.

In autumn we have an appetite for mushrooms and oily fish.

EAT *SOBA*

Soba is a healthy food that is very popular in Japan. Even pasta lovers eat these noodles.

I was watching Rachael Ray on her TV cooking show one day and I saw that she was using Japanese *soba* for shrimp and vegetable pasta. "It is a very healthy noodle," she said.

Soba is a type of thin Japanese noodle made from buckwheat. It is known as a low-calorie food. When I was working in Japan, my coworker was always having *soba* for lunch. "I have to lose 5 pounds in two months. My friend told me *soba* helps you lose weight, so I'm trying it."

A serving of rice has 165 calories, bread has 260, and *soba* has 130.

Not only is it low calorie, it is also good for blood pressure. My friend lost more than 5 pounds before her wedding. Well, she did a lot of exercise, too.

TOFU FOR PROTEIN

Tofu has become as popular in the world as sushi, I think. My grandfather had diabetes, so on his doctor's advice, he ate tofu every day until he died at a ripe old age. Our family believes that tofu equals good nutrition and good health. I serve it almost every day.

These days I study about its benefits. Tofu is low in calories, contains beneficial amounts of iron, and has no cholesterol (a risk factor for heart disease). Depending on the coagulant used in manufacturing, the tofu may also be high in calcium (important for bone development and maintenance) and magnesium (especially important for athletes). Tofu is relatively high in protein: about 10.7% for firm tofu and 5.3% for the "silky" kind. In 1998, the FDA announced that soy protein may reduce cholesterol and the risk of heart disease.

How to Eat Tofu

Have you ever eaten tofu? The simplest way is just take it out of the package, put it on a plate, and eat it a small bit at a time.

The Japanese way is to sprinkle on dried fish flakes and diced green onion, then pour a little soy sauce over it. If you want a more American taste, you can use it instead of ground beef to make a tofuburger.

EAT MARINE VEGETABLES EVERY DAY (SEAWEED, *WAKAME*, *KONBU*, *TORORO*, *UZUKI*)

Seaweed, *wakame*, *konbu*, *tororo*, *uzuki*? If you have never had these foods, you might feel weird tasting them for the first time.

Mary and I went to a Japanese restaurant together. They served us *wakame* miso soup with the meal.

She was just staring at the black stuff in the soup, and then she picked it out of the bowl and put it in another dish.

"I can't eat that weird stuff," she protested. But I told her just to try it, that it was a kind of seaweed and that she might like it.

I think people are afraid to put strange-looking food in their mouths.

Sushi is eaten all over the world now, but not so long ago people said to me, "Japanese can eat black paper? Are they crazy? Oh, yuck!"

Times have changed. Eating sushi has become a symbol of sophistication.

Now, *wakame* has also hit the spotlight in America. Fucoxanthin, recently discovered by Japanese scientists, has been extracted from *wakame* seaweed that grows freely in the Sea of Japan. Fucoxanthin has been clinically tested, and new studies conducted at Hokkaido University have found that fucoxanthin can help burn fatty tissue. Studies in mice have shown that fucoxanthin induces expression of the fat-burning protein that accumulates in fat tissue around the internal organs. Expression of protein was significantly increased in mice fed fucoxanthin.

Wakame is also used in topical beauty treatments.

In traditional Eastern medicine, it has been used for blood purification, intestinal strength, skin, hair, reproductive organs, and menstrual regularity.

MORE ABOUT *KONBU*

Konbu is used in Japanese cuisine. It's the main ingredient in a standard soup stock called *dashi*. *Konbu* (also written *kombu*) is sold dried or pickled in vinegar.

To make the *dashi* soup stock, put a strip of dried *konbu* in cold water and bring the pot to a boil.

Konbu is a good source of glutamic acid, an amino acid responsible for the "savory" taste the Japanese call *umami*. In 1908 the Japanese officially added *umami* as one of the basic taste categories, in addition to salty, sweet, sour, and bitter.

3

nimble ninja

INTRODUCTION

Life expectancy for Japanese women is eighty-six years, and for men, it's eighty years.

This is the longest life expectancy in the world.

There are many reasons for Japanese longevity, but one factor is the everyday lifestyle.

The majority of people over seventy years old can't drive a car. They grew up without cars and never learned to drive as adults.

So anywhere they go, they have to walk or ride a bicycle. My mother's neighbor in Japan is eighty-eight years old. He goes shopping 2 miles away from home by bicycle every day. Haru, who is ninety-one years old, walks a mile to see her doctor.

Taking care of houseplants or light gardening of vegetables and herbs is thought to be imbued with spirituality, and offers the chance for fresh air and outdoor exercise.

Housekeeping includes folding the futon, hanging laundry, and sweeping the floor, all of which burn calories and keep muscles toned.

The traditional ways keep people active, sharp, and involved in their own lives, so they see no reason to do things differently.

Everyday life includes enough exercise, so most people don't need to make a special effort to do much more.

I hope you can find your own easy exercise, something you can enjoy and do often to keep healthy.

RIDE A BICYCLE

Before I started to drive a car, my bicycle was my auto.

Come rain or shine, sleet or snow, I would just hop on and sit in the little seat and move my legs around and around. And you know what? I always got where I needed to go. I didn't melt in the sun or freeze in the cold or blow away in the wind.

The little basket attached to the handlebars was plenty big enough to hold what I had bought. If you make short trips every day to local stores on your bike, you don't need a big trunk to haul big bags or boxes.

You don't need any gas or major maintenance. Parking is easy and FREE. And best of all, it is good exercise—not hard exercise—just good for everyone big and small, old and young.

TAKE THE STAIRS

People commute on public transportation in Japan: subways, trains, and busses. Most everyone has to walk to the nearest station, which is often a half-mile or more away from home. And most stations have long flights of steps that take you up and over the tracks.

To get to the subway, you have to descend long flights of stairs that take you deep underground. It's not so bad going all the way down the steps, but going up feels like a 5-mile jog. Your heart beats fast, and your leg muscles tighten, but you just keep going to get back up to street level again.

Fortunately for me, during the past five years, most stations and other public places have installed escalators. Still, some of them haven't. It's harder for the elderly people, but I think they do better than I do when it comes to climbing up all those steps.

One day when I was back in Japan on vacation, I met five elderly neighbor ladies at the station near my home in a suburb of Tokyo. They are all over eighty-five, but none of them has a problem walking up all the steps and getting on the train.

"Where are you going now?" I asked one of them.

"We are going to see a musical variety show at city hall."

We got off at the same station. They were fine going up the stairs, but I didn't feel like it, so I used the escalator. One of the grannies saw me and said, "You are still young. You have to use your legs, otherwise you will have a miserable old age."

I guess I got used to the American lifestyle. Everyday life revolves around getting in the car and driving all over. I almost never walk a mile at a time, and for that reason, I can't beat the old Japanese grannies up the steps at the train station.

So you see, it's not only food that contributes to long life in Japan. The other part is a healthy, everyday lifestyle. All research shows the benefits of walking, and exercise of any kind is highly recommended.

EXERCISE IN YOUR CHAIR

When I was working at an advertising company, our art director had a minor heart attack when he was forty-six years old. After that he started doing this sitting and exercising routine in the office every day at 3:00 pm. I asked him how to do it. A couple weeks later he gave me some illustrations.

twist

flex

bend

MOVE, STRETCH, AND REACH WHILE KEEPING HOUSE

The Japanese lifestyle gives us an automatic workout all day from morning to night.

Hoisting and Hefting the Futon

In the morning we have to remove the futon from the floor on which we slept, and fold it up and put it away. Because most Japanese homes or condos are small, the same space that's used for daytime living is used for sleeping at night. Compare it to a New York apartment with a hideaway bed in the wall. The difference is we keep a fold-up futon in a compact, specially designed closet in the daytime, and take it out and lay it open on the floor at night to sleep. In the morning, we lift it up and put it away in the closet along with the blankets and pillows.

Many people sleep in a futon instead of a bed in Japan. These futons are different from the American ones because there is no wooden frame. They are stuffed with light, 100% cotton.

On sunny days, we hang the futon outside to make it fluffy and dry. The sunshine kills the bacteria.

But we have to hang up the futon on a pole or over the deck railing. This is a kind of regular workout routine.

One futon may weigh up to 20 pounds. Folding and lifting requires using the muscles of the whole body.

Laundry

The Japanese laundry room is usually next to the bathroom. It's common for most people to soak in a hot bathtub at night and keep the warm water in it until morning. Often the bath water is used for laundry. Remember, Japanese people shower and rinse before getting in the deep tub, so the water is relatively clean.

Just dip a small bucket into the tub, fill it several times, and pour the water into the clothes washer. The result: save water— as well as gas or electricity, because the water is already warm.

If there is room in the back yard, deck, or balcony, we can hang the clothes outside to dry. More work and lifting!

Dusting and Straightening Up

Before vacuuming, we use a cloth attached to a long broom or mop handle to take out dust and cobwebs from ceiling to floor.

You have to stretch your muscles to do this. Then you're ready to vacuum.

One thing we do that helps keep the floors clean is take off our shoes in the entryway, which is usually a step below floor level, so a lot of dirt and dust just stays there at the front door.

It's a good idea to sweep away dust in the entrance every day to keep dust from being blown into the house.

Grandma always said, "The entrance reflects how your family lives. It's like a mirror. It has to be clean and neat because when guests arrive, they form a first impression about you and your house right there."

Therefore, when our family lived with Grandma, she disciplined us to change our habits.

My husband is 5 feet 11 inches tall (180 cm). Somehow it

was hard for him when coming home to bend way down and put his shoes together neatly. This custom was odd for him at the beginning of his life in Japan.

He left his shoes messy and scattered. Right and left were not lined up. Grandma did not like that, so she would always bend over and stretch to straighten them up. This was her exercise.

According to an American Heart Association report done on 302 adults in their seventies and eighties, just by vacuuming, mopping floors, washing windows, and so forth for a little more than an hour a day, a person can burn about 285 calories, lowering the risk of death by 30%!

GARDEN IN A 1-SQUARE-METER AREA EVERY DAY

Blue sky, fresh air, the smell of ripened vegetables, the sweet smell of flowers—all of this gives strength to body, mind, and soul. You start to dig, plant, and water. You pull the weeds and tend to your flowers and vegetables. This is fairly easy outdoor exercise, under the sun and in the fresh air.

Gardening just feels good. You feel productive. It gives you something you can see and touch. Your small crop is growing from your efforts.

It may seem like a small thing, but working with nature can teach us simple important things.

Many Japanese cities recommend gardening, but available

open land is scarce, so the city offers a 1- square-meter area (about 10 square feet) to each family that wants to plant a garden, and they can grow anything they like.

On weekends, families can go to these gardens and tend to their organic vegetables.

This is family time. It is also a time when you can talk to other people about your crop, sharing information and building community.

". . . ING" AND SQUAT

This easy exercise is one you can do at home, work, or almost anywhere.

My friend looks twenty years younger than her age. She has a very nice shape.

She doesn't have a professional trainer. She is only doing ". . . ing" and squat.

What is that?

Just ". . . ing" and squat.

When she is cooking, she goes up and down on her heels twenty times.

Brushing her teeth: ten times.

Watching TV: twenty times.

Standing and waiting to cross

the street: ten times up and down on the heels and toes and ten half-squats.

You can find any "...ing" and squat combination.

EXERCISE IN THE CAR

If you commute by car, you are sitting down for quite a long time, maybe for more than 2 hours a day. Here are some easy ways to relax and release tension while you are behind the wheel.

- Isometrics: Hold your breath and tighten your stomach muscles for 5 to 10 seconds, then relax and exhale. Repeat 10–15 times. This can help flatten your stomach and improve your posture.
- Neck exercise: While waiting for the signal to change, move your neck slowly right and left. Don't hurry or jerk your neck back and forth.
- Shoulder exercise: Put your left hand on your right shoulder and massage with your fingertips. Then repeat, this time with your right hand on your left shoulder. You can use a similar right/left procedure to pat or slap your shoulders for the same relaxing effect.
- Back exercise: Straighten your back and press it against the car seat, then tighten up the stomach for a few seconds. Repeat a few

times. When you get out of the car, go around to the rear, extend your arms out straight, place your hands firmly on the trunk, and bend forward from the waist.

- Whole body exercise 1: Park your car in the farthest spot away from the store when you are running errands
- Whole body exercise 2: Wash your car yourself! You will bend and stretch and use muscles all over your body

WALK, WALK, WALK!

Every time I go to Japan, I see an increasing number of older people, especially in the daytime. I notice them on the trains, in the malls, and at the supermarkets. I see more elderly people than young people.

According to a source at the United Nations in 2002, the percentage of the population over sixty years of age will be 22.8% in the US and 33.7% in Japan by the year 2020.

One thing that impresses me is that so many seniors are physically active. They get up and get out of the house early on. They put on a hat to protect their head and skin from the sun. It does not matter which season. They put on their hat and out the door they go. Also, they wear comfortable walking shoes and wear a small backpack to keep their hands free to walk.

For most people, everywhere you go, you just walk, walk,

walk! When I was growing up in Japan in the 1960s, only upper-class people had cars. But now Japan is like America; every household has a car. But in Japan, most people use their car only on weekends. During the week, they commute on public transportation: subways, trains, and busses. Most everyone has to walk to the nearest station, which can be a half-mile or more away from home.

My family and friends all wear a walk-o-meter or *man po kei*, which is a 10,000-step pedometer. They keep track of how much they walk.

The health department recommends 10,000 steps per day to lower blood pressure and cholesterol. Walking 10,000 steps burns 300 calories. When you burn more calories than you take in, you will lose weight. This is the ideal exercise!!

This walk-o-meter became popular forty years ago. I use it every day now, but it is hard to get up to 10,000 steps.

According to Japanese research, male office workers average 3,800 steps a day, and housewives only 2,800 steps. But people keep wearing the walk-o-meter and shoot for the goal.

The American lifestyle centers around the automobile. The Japanese base theirs on walking, so seniors in Japan don't have to make up reasons to exercise because it is part of everyday life, and it keeps them slim and healthy

I think it makes sense to set a goal for how many steps to take every day. For me it emphasizes the quality of the time I use for walking. I take more steps on purpose and avoid shortcuts because I've made up my own goal for the day. You don't need to buy fancy equipment or spend a lot of money on accessories to lose weight. Just walk it off.

JAPANESE SANDALS MASSAGE THE FEET AND MEND THE MIND

My son's friend Shin was born in Japan to a Japanese father and a Caucasian-American mother. Because of his dad's work, his family moved around to several different countries while he was growing up. He chose to go to college in America and graduated from an East Coast college. When he was in school, he once came to visit us in San Francisco during winter break.

I was surprised to see that he was wearing *geta* sandals without any socks. It was cold and rainy that January in northern California, but no matter to him. He said he even wears *geta* on cold, snowy days in Washington, D.C. In fact, he said he wore only *geta* all year long. I asked him why.

"Because it's good for my health and stimulates the brain."

Have you ever seen *geta*? They are flat wooden sandals with a fabric thong. There are two strong strips of wood on the bottom to raise the foot well above the ground. Traditionally, they are worn with *yukata* (light cotton kimono) in summer. Of course, you can wear them with Western clothes, just as Shin does, even in rain or snow to keep the feet dry.

Sumo wrestlers, who still walk about town in traditional

Japanese dress, wear *geta* all the time, but most people don't. They are really a thing of the past.

But *geta* massage the acupressure points on the bottom of the feet, and, therefore, play a part in natural, preventive health practices. The focus of the acupressure aids proper functioning of the vital internal organs, and according to Shin (and other researchers), you don't feel as tired at the end of a busy day. Perhaps best of all, the neural pathways of the brain get stimulated.

Looking for better memory? Feelings of well-being? Put on a pair of *geta* and take a "clack-clack" walk down the street.

JAPANESE REFLEXOLOGY: BAMBOO

This section has nothing to do with a bamboo floor. I want to tell you about a kind of foot massager you can use yourself. It is very popular now in Japan, where even fitness clubs recommend it to their members for easy, beneficial exercise.

Reflexology is a kind of massage applied to the feet or hands. Japanese people have long believed in the benefits of this kind of bamboo massager for three reasons:

1. The foot has an important link to the heart. There are many pressure points in the foot that, when pushed or massaged, can stimulate heart health, but normally you cannot stimulate them by yourself. The bamboo massager helps generate good energy flow from your feet.

Our ancestors believed this kind of foot massage could rid the body and mind of ills and bad spirits and bring good luck.

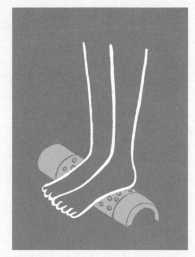

2. The massage involves active exercise as well. because you have to stand and move your weight back and forth, stretching the Achilles tendon. If you train the arches of the feet (*tsuchifumazu*), you can learn to walk straight with good posture.

3. Bamboo foot reflexology speeds up blood circulation, bringing a sense of warmth and comfort to the body.

BREATHING

Take a big, deep breath with your arms wide open and breathe out while closing your arms in.

This simple exercise can calm you down as it fills your lungs with much needed extra air.

Deep breathing is generally a more effective way to ingest more oxygen. It is often used as a therapy for anxiety. A com-

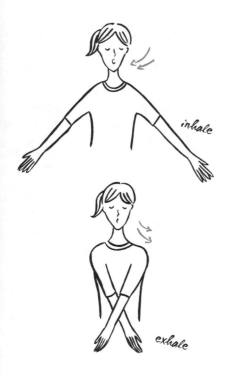

inhale

exhale

mon diaphragmatic breathing exercise is as follows:

1. Sit or lie comfortably, wearing loose garments.
2. Extend your arms and cross them in front of you.
3. Open your arms wide and slowly inhale through your nose or through pursed lips (to slow down the intake of breath).
4. As you inhale, feel your stomach expand. If your chest expands, focus on breathing with your diaphragm.
5. As you bring your arms back to the crossed position, slowly exhale through pursed lips to regulate the release of air.
6. Rest and repeat.

4

green tea therapy

INTRODUCTION

Each generation comes up with new and different ways to relax.

In Japan, karaoke, video games, animation, pachinko, and manga are all things the young generation does to have fun and forget the stresses of the real world. The dictionary defines relaxation as "the art and science of doing nothing." So, for the rest of us, what is the "nothing" we can do to relax?

According to Japanese medical researchers, good health and longevity may be related, among other activities, to taking relaxing baths. Japanese people like thumb baths, footbaths, sake baths, and especially the *onsen*, which is a hot spring or mineral bath.

Bathing is not only for old people. Young and old alike enjoy it. The ultimate *onsen* experience is to soak the body in an outdoor hot spring on a snowy day. You feel the cold air nipping at your face, yet you are turning red with the warmth of the bubbling water. The evergreens around you droop with heavy snow and ice. You can see the ocean far below. You close your eyes and think of—nothing. The heartbeat slows.

What about the "nothingness" of Zen? Go to the temple for prayer and meditation, and you are surrounded by the sweet smells of incense. Body and mind connect. Alternative physical and spiritual treatments include *shiatsu*, *reiki*, acupuncture, and more.

Your body responds with calm.

Calmness is one key to good health, says Dr. Herbert Benson of the Mind/Body Institute at Harvard Medical School. During the relaxation response, blood pressure is lower, and metabolic rate, heartbeat, and breathing each slow down.

Can you think of nothing?

THUMB BATH

If you are sitting or standing in the same position for a long time, your muscles get tense. You feel tired. Your nerves are strained. You may have a headache or body aches. Your mind is dull. Here's something you can do, a thumb bath:

1. Put warm water into two teacups. Soak each of your thumbs in each separate cup.
2. Take deep breaths, and count to sixty or any number you like.

Soaking your thumbs in the hot water may relieve some of your tension and get rid of stress.

GAZING AT THE CHANGES IN THE SEASONS

Each of the four seasons in Japan is dramatically different from the others.

Throughout history, people have found ways to celebrate the seasons, and today groups like Friends of the Earth hold special events based on those centuries-old traditions in order to help us feel closer to nature and to the natural cycles of change throughout each year.

Japan has numerous seasonal traditions, for example *ohanami* in spring, *hanabi* in summer, *momiji gari* in autumn, and in winter, *yukimi*.

- *Ohanami:* In spring we notice the flowers bursting into bloom, especially the cherry blossoms, which are the sweet symbol for spring. *Ohanami* is the day when you go to view the cherry blossoms under the cherry tree. It's a time of pure indulgence. You recline on a blanket or mat, open up your *bento* box, and feast on a dozen delectable delicacies served with rice. You drink sake or beer and sing along to karaoke.
- *Hanabi:* In summer, people go to see *hanabi* (fireworks). It's like the Fourth of July in America. The difference is that in Japan the fireworks go on all summer long. They are held at different locations and on different dates, so you can choose to go watch as many times as you want.
- *Momiji gari:* In autumn, the leaves change to burning reds, oranges, and gold. People march upon the mountainsides in search of the most dazzling tableaux.
- *Yukimi:* In winter, people make art from snow, and show it off to the public.

Think of all the different ways you can celebrate nature throughout the seasons. During each season, take careful note of changes in color and texture, and create special events for gazing at nature's displays. How simple! Family and friends get together, go off to a park or mountainside or to the shore, bring some potluck, and just let nature put on her show.

FOOTBATHS

A footbath is really very relaxing.

If you are characteristically cold, I recommend it as an easy way to relax and warm up.

When you don't feel like taking a bath or shower, you can take a footbath.

Choose a container big enough to put both feet in.

Into the container, pour hot or warm water, then set the container inside a big garbage bag to keep the warmth and steam from escaping.

If the hot water begins to cool off, just add more hot water. You can decide what temperature is comfortable for you.

A footbath may relieve

a headache, stomachache, or coughing. Perhaps the best time to take a footbath is at night before you go to bed. Your feet will be nice and warm, tension and stress will be released, and you will sleep well.

FORTUNE-TELLERS (URANAI)

When you are confused, depressed or sad, what do you do?

Maybe your concerns take you to a therapist?

In the cities of Japan, there are sidewalk fortune-tellers on almost every block.

Their signs read "URANAI [fortune-teller]: I can give you advice for your health, career, marriage, divorce , whatever."

The average cost for each reading is $30 to $50. The fortune-teller will read the lines in the palm of your hand or chart your course from your date of birth. She usually encourages you to hang in there, or predicts that some good or bad fortune is coming sooner or later. People say it feels safe and secure, since the fortune-teller is a total stranger, someone you will probably never meet again, so you can relax and talk candidly about your problems.

In America, it is so different. You have the psychologist Dr. Phil on TV every day.

In Japan, the fortune-teller Ms. Hosoki had her own show. The show was a big hit. It dealt with people's problems.

People want to understand why bad things happen to them. They want to have answers.

Another phenomenon in Japan is bestselling books that explain personality based on blood type.

People who believe in this explanation understand the attitudes and actions of others by their blood type. As blood type represetnts the chemistry of a person's body, it can indicate personality as well:

- Type A: serious, anxious, reserved
- Type B: carefree, self-absorbed, independent
- Type AB: unique, flamboyant, curious
- Type O: very friendly, kind, good leader, messy

It is said that if you cannot control something, you can learn to accept it. So when we make an effort to accept a problem that we always have with other individuals, we want to have an explanation. If we say, "It's his blood type," everyone agrees. It's a simple solution for a complicated problem. You relax and accept, and forget about your differences for a while.

MALE \ FEMALE	A	B	O	AB
A	AA	AB	AO	A AB
	75%	50%	80%	65%
B	BA	BB	BO	B AB
	60%	75%	75%	90%
O	OA	OB	OO	O AB
	95%	60%	65%	60%
AB	AB A	AB B	AB O	AB AB
	40%	80%	50%	70%

some believe that the chances of a man and woman being compatible can be predicted by their blood types; do you agree?

SPAS AND HOT SPRINGS

You can relax at home by meditating.

But if you go to an *onsen*, you really relax both physically and mentally.

What is an *onsen*? An *onsen* is a natural hot spring bath heated by geothermal energy. The volcanic nature provides plenty of hot water containing minerals such as sulphur, sodium chloride, iron, and hydrogen carbonate.

Doctors and scientists believe these natural elements have various medical benefits.

When Grandma was a teenager, she had rheumatic fever. That was during the Meiji period, just before the turn of the twentieth century. She stayed at an *onsen* spa for six months. Medical treatments incorporated the healing powers of nature, along with the few chemical drug therapies that were available at the time.

Onsen therapy required a good soak in the right hot spring to heal specific aches and pains and to treat other illnesses such as arthralgia, chronic skin diseases, diabetes, constipation, menstrual disorders, and so on.

So, according to Grandma, the six-month *onsen* therapy helped to nurse her back to good health. Living long, until the age of ninety-four, and with visits to the doctor few and far between, she followed the old way using the powers of natural healing and good nutrition.

Just like Grandma, I go to the *onsen* to soak in the steamy hot mineral baths. My aches and pains are relieved, and by the end of my stay, my skin is rejuvenated and smooth.

I really love going to the outdoor *onsen* in early spring.

As is our custom, I slip naked into the hot pool. Surrounding me may be little clumps of winter snow in the trees and on the ground, but nearby the palm flowers have begun to bloom.

So cold, yet so warm in the bath, I look out upon nature. I contemplate winter melting into spring. I simply relax and let my mind drift far away from the real world.

JAPANESE INCENSE *(SENKO)*

Every time I go to a Japanese temple, I find calm. One reason is the burning of Japanese incense.

Inside the temple is a blend of natural light and candlelight, and the spirals of smoke from the incense permeate the air.

I sit in front of the Buddha and take in the light and the fragrances. These are not Western smells.

For centuries, incense has been burned by Zen Buddhist priests, who say it is part of their meditative ritual. This may be because some incense includes citronella, which repels mosquitoes and other aggravating pests. The incense is thus designed to prevent bothersome insects from distracting practitioners.

There are two important ingredients in incense. One is agarwood (*jinko*), and the other is sandalwood (*byakudan*). These give off the most calming aromas and lend themselves well to meditation.

If the stresses of life are getting to you, try the aromatic therapy of Japanese incense.

RELAXATION: LISTENING TO NATURE

When you go out into nature, listen to the sounds.

Birds. Wind. Animals. Water Insects.

I heard from a friend, an American poet, that Japanese hear nature differently. Can you hear what they hear?

A bush warbler sings "Ho-ho-kekyo," announcing spring is here.

In the summer time cicadas drone "Min-min-min." It's hot!

The autumn crickets chirp "Ri-n, ri-n." It's getting cooler.

Nature speaks.

Water hits rocks: music.

The wind blows through all four seasons. The traditional instruments—bamboo flute, *taiko*, *koto*, and *shamisen*—mimic the melodies as the seasons change.

Sounds of nature have healing tones.

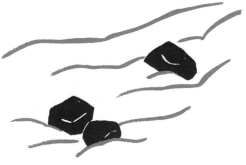

REIKI

Once I received a gift certificate for a free *reiki* session for my birthday. The *reiki* master was located here in our town in California. The e-mail describing *reiki* said, "If you are stressed out, a *reiki* session will relax you through spiritual power." I really didn't know what *reiki* was, even though it comes from Japan. The *reiki* therapist was an American woman who had been trained in San Francisco. I had somehow expected that she would be Japanese. After I saw her *reiki* certification hanging on the wall, I understood better, and realized I'd heard about this before.

Reiki was discovered by Mikao Usui in1922 after a twenty-one-day retreat on Mount Kurama involving meditation, fasting, and prayer.

Usui said that by mystical revelation he had gained knowledge of a spiritual power to transfer and attune to others.

The treatment was interesting. The therapist's hands became very warm, almost hot. She said this was the manifestation of the healing energy that entered into her body. She placed the palms of her hands on different areas of my body. During the session, I felt a lightness in my body. Tightness and tension were gone. By the time it was over, my energy level was high and my emotions were calm.

Reiki has five principles:

1. Do not be angry.
2. Do not worry.
3. Be grateful.
4. Work with integrity.
5. Be kind to others.

Every morning and every night, sit in the *gassho* position (hands held palm-to-palm in front of your chest) and speak these words out loud from your heart. You will connect to a higher spiritual power.

The five principles work for me.

SAKE BATH

After long working hours, soaking in a deep, hot bath up to your shoulders is very relaxing.

Have you heard of a sake *furo* (sake bath)?

It is popular with Japanese for beauty and health.

Sake is an alcoholic beverage made from rice.

Sake in hot bathwater keeps you warm for a long time. Therefore, the hot soak before bedtime can lull you into tranquil-

ity and lead you to a good night's sleep.

The sake bath also smoothes and moisturizes your skin, and helps your skin shed dead, flaky skin cells.

This is

because *koji-kin* (*aspergillus oryzae*), the mold used to break down the sake rice for fermentation, is working on the skin.

If you like singing in the shower, you can sing karaoke in the bath, too. Just let yourself go.

Here is how to make a sake bath:

1. Heat up the bathwater to about 100°F (38°C) and add 4 cups of sake.
2. Soak for as long as you like. After the bath, rinse well and dry.
3. Enjoy the warm, silky feel of smooth skin.

SHIATSU (JAPANESE FINGER PRESSURE)

Shoulder aches, neck aches, muscle aches, back aches—aches and pains can affect any part of the body. There may be no medical evidence, but it seems to me that Japanese people may be even more sensitive to these pains than others.

Go to the drugstore and you will see so many remedies for muscle pain: *tokuhon* (an analgesic patch), magnets, ointments, "Oriental" herbs. . . . Japanese have been using *tokuhon* for more than a hundred years for pain relief for any part of the body. And it does help.

Nowadays, *shiatsu* is preferred by many. This is called finger massage or acupressure in English. In Tokyo, inside station buildings or close to any train station, you'll find a *shiatsu* clinic.

Busy city people seek relief from tension. The *shiatsu* therapist pushes his fingers deep into achy muscles. The pressure is hard, but it feels so good because the therapist knows exactly which points to stimulate. It used to be that only middle-aged or old people went for *shiatsu* treatments, but now young people who sit at computers all day need to loosen up their stiff muscles. Some clinics in or near a station offer 10 minutes for $10, which isn't bad for the young on the run.

YUTANPO

A *yutanpo* is the Japanese version of a hot-water bottle.

It is about 12 inches (30 cm) long and 10 inches (25 cm) wide, and holds about 3 quarts (3 liters) of hot water.

When I was young, we did not have an electric heating system. In the winter, even the inside of the bed was cold. Most families used a *yutanpo* to keep the feet warm under the covers. It feels so cozy and peaceful, especially when it's snowy or cold or rainy at night. You can stay warm all night without using an electric blanket or artificial heat, so your skin doesn't dry up. The next morning, you can use the water from the bottle to wash your face. The original *yutanpo* was made of tin. Nowadays many different materials are used.

During the past couple years, the *yutanpo* has become popular again because it provides natural heat for the body.

After boiling water, add it carefully to the *yutanpo*; then cork the *yutanpo* tightly and slide it into a fabric bag. Then place the bag underneath your bedcovers to keep you warm.

You can also make one of your own by reusing a plastic

put the bottle in a plastic bag to prevent leakage

wrap the bottle in a towel to prevent burning

bottle and wrapping it up in a towel. (See "Recycling and Reusing.")

It's a green tea idea for a cold night!

ZAZEN

Zen is the most widely practiced form of meditation in Japan.

The core of Zen practice is the sitting position. It is called *zazen* in Japanese. *Zazen* includes a couple ways of sitting, known as postures. The *seiza* posture is sitting with your back erect and your legs folded beneath you, but you can also sit with your legs crossed. Usually, you sit on a *zabuton*, which is a large square or round cushion placed on a padded mat. Even so, it may feel more hard than soft.

The point of sitting on the floor and facing the center of the room is to regulate the mind. Awareness is directed toward counting or watching the breath or centering the flow of energy toward the navel. A primary rule of practice is meditation with no objects or anchors. Just concentrate on the breath.

Zen experts recommend 5 or 10 minutes of daily practice.

Zen teaches that the ego will naturally resist the spirit, so discipline and regularity of practice are important for progress.

GREEN TEA CUP AND HAPPINESS

I have a green tea cup given to me by my uncle in Japan. On it is written ten ways to be a happy person. When I drink green tea I always read it. This helps relax and refresh me:

1. Appreciate what you get.
2. Live within your means.
3. Keep good relations with your partner.
4. Take good care of your possessions.
5. Stay healthy.
6. Be honest.
7. Think of your job as a hobby.
8. Follow your dream.
9. Admit when you are wrong.
10. Give from your heart.

5

geisha beauty

INTRODUCTION

I start each day with a cup of green tea in the morning.

After that I use a green tea pack on my face for about 10 minutes.

Then I take a shower, washing with bamboo charcoal soap and shampoo.

For conditioner, I use a solution of vinegar, water, and rosemary.

Before sleeping, I take off my makeup with olive oil from the kitchen.

Once a week I give myself an anti-wrinkle treatment with egg-shell membrane.

I don't use cosmetics for basic skincare anymore.

My beautician in Japan has known my hair and skin for over twenty years. She hadn't seen me for quite a while and said, "Your hair looks so good—so shiny and healthy. Not only that, your skin has improved a lot. What's your secret? American cosmetics? I'd like to buy some!"

I told her about the organic products I use every day.

The next time I met her she expressed her appreciation to me. The tips I gave her really work for her, too.

This organic cosmetic care makes me feel so much better.

Not only that, I save close to $100 a month.

Looking good is not a luxury now. It's just part of my daily, eco-friendly routine.

VINEGAR CONDITIONER FOR VERY SHINY HAIR

I like to use safe and comfortable beauty items every day.

Did you know you can make conditioner without spending extra money?

This conditioner makes your hair soft, smooth, and shiny. It's made of vinegar and herbs. Preparation is very simple.

1. Take an empty clear plastic shampoo or conditioner bottle and put in about 16 ounces (500 cc) of water.
2. Add 4 tablespoons of white vinegar or rice vinegar.
3. Drop in 3 to 4 pieces of garden-fresh rosemary or sage.
4. You'll need to modify the procedure if you use dried herbs: Boil them in 2 cups (500 cc) of water. Drain the water into a bowl, and let it cool off. Then pour in 3 big spoonfuls of vinegar. You can now funnel the liquid into the plastic bottle.

This conditioner really works, and the amount you make lasts two to three weeks. I found that my hair is not only shiny and soft, but I also have less dandruff and less hair loss. The color of my hair dye lasts longer, too. You will be delighted with the lustrous look of your hair.

EGG WHITE FACE MASK

If you have dry skin or dark spots (small blackheads) around your nose, try an egg white mask to moisturize and cleanse.

1. Separate the white from the yolk of the egg.
2. Make a meringue by whipping the white until it's stiff.
3. Rub it on your face.
4. Wait 5 to 10 minutes.
5. Before it dries, wash it all off.

There's a bonus ingredient, too. Use the membrane on the inside of the egg-shell to cover any wrinkles before you put on the pack.

HONEY FOR CHAPPED LIPS

In the winter, when freezing wind or cold makes your lips dry and chapped, put honey on them.

Honey is a gentle cure, and it brightens up your lips as well.

Not only that, it tastes good. Sweet!

You also can make a great facial and body pack from honey. My friend Junko learned this from her grandmother.

I use it, too. It makes my skin satiny smooth. I think the result is amazing.

You will need these ingredients to mix up in a Tupperware bowl. If it is not smooth, add one more tablespoon of honey:

- 1 egg white
- 3 tablespoons honey
- 1 cup Epsom salts

Let the mixture stand 1 hour at room temperature.

Just apply 1 tablespoon on your chin for 30 seconds and completely wash it off. After that, try it on your body. If you like the results, try it on your whole face.

A HOT TOWEL TO REFRESH YOUR SKIN

When your face looks tired, you'll have trouble getting the best results from your make-up.

Place a hot towel over your face. It makes your skin relax.

Do this before washing your face with soap. You can heat up the towel with hot water or steam.

The capillaries under your skin will swell up and stimulate a rosy glow on your face. Once you are glowing, put some moisturizer on with cotton puffs, gently patting your skin. You will notice your skin is refreshed and ready for makeup, if you wish.

Another way to revive your skin is to steam your face without applying the towel directly. Put hot water in a bowl. Cover your head and the steaming bowl of hot water with a towel, using the towel to trap the steam around your face.

OLIVE OIL FOR DRY SKIN

Olive oil is not only for cooking. It's good for your skin, too.

I use it to remove makeup before going to sleep at night. It completely cleans off the makeup and moisturizes the skin. I usually don't have to use anything else. I can just then go to bed.

By the way, there is a reason that olive oil will help your skin. Olive oil has Vitamins A, E, and D. These nutrients change dry skin to healthy, moisturized skin.

Olive oil was used for cosmetic care as long as 4,000 years ago in ancient Egypt. One reason is that it lasts a very long time without spoiling. The Egyptians used it to protect against sun burn, and you can use it for the same purpose or, even better, use it to remove foundation or eye make-up. Always use extra virgin olive oil, which is thick and rich.

SILK GLOVES FOR SKIN CARE: GEISHA SKIN

Once you have silk clothes, you will wear them again and again because they are very light and warm. Silk feels good on the skin.

My friend's skin is very smooth and shiny, like silk. I asked her what her beauty secret is. She said it is the Geisha Way.

She uses a silk glove for cleansing her body. She does not use soap or anything else.

If you'd like to try it, use a silk glove or cloth on your face, body, ears, lips, and everywhere else. As I said, no soap or body wash, just cleanse with the silk. A glove makes it easy to clean small body parts, like toes and fingers and behind the ears and around the nose.

The best way to do this is to place your hand in the glove and then gently stroke the glove over your skin as you stand in the shower.

The prickly substance sebum, which can damage the skin, is scraped away by the silk. That's why silk can polish your skin. Even wearing silk clothes is good for the body.

But try not to wash too hard. If you scrub hard, your skin may get red and dry. For the best results, move the silk glove softly over the skin.

MILK AND TEA TO RELIEVE SUNBURN

When you don't have any after-sun lotion, try this.

Just put cold milk on a cotton puff and dab it on the skin.

Or you can put a green tea pack on your face to cool off.

This is good not only for sunburn, but also for getting rid of pimples and freckles.

You can also use cold green tea bags as a kind of compress to help relieve tired eyes. In winter, your skin may get dry and rough. You can make a milk and warm water mixture to soak your skin. Your skin will feel smooooooth.

FACIAL MASSAGE WITH TEASPOON

A teaspoon for a facial?

When I saw someone patting her face with a spoon on a TV show in Japan, I couldn't imagine what she was doing. She said this makes your skin look healthy and your color vivid.

Patting your face with a spoon shrinks the capillaries.

1. Hold the spoon handle.
2. Pat your face with the spoon from center to side, lightly and rhythmically.

3. Do the same from bottom to top.
4. Pat for 3 minutes.

The capillaries allow the flow of oxygen in the blood again. Any pallor from lack of sleep or swelling disappears.

CUCUMBER MASSAGE FOR SKIN

I still remember my mother using a cucumber face pack. She told me it was the best moisturizer for her skin. It really helps to rejuvenate it, especially if your skin looks tired and pale.

Just cut some slices of cucumber, lie back, and put them on your face.

Cucumber slices are also good for relieving puffy eyes.

Close your eyes, and place a slice over each eyelid for tired eyes. Leave them for 10 to 15 minutes while you rest.

(Test on your arm first to make sure you're not allergic!)

HOMEMADE LOTION FROM THE KITCHEN

When I looked at my mother's and Grandma's faces, I noticed that they didn't have many age spots or wrinkles, and I was always wondering why, because they never used any expensive cosmetics. My mother uses only foundation.

As for me, I had serious skin trouble after I turned forty here in California. There's a lot of sunshine here, along with low humidity and brisk winds.

My skin turned dry and I got a lot of wrinkles and spots on my face. I thought I looked ten years older than I really was.

I tried many cosmetics and spent a lot of money, but nothing worked well.

So I asked my mother what she was using for skin care.

She said she makes several different kinds of lotions from her garden and kitchen.

I began making and using them. Three months later, my face was much improved.

People asked what I was using. I always said, "It's organic!"

Here are my secret handmade lotions. I give exact formulas and sometimes the amounts involved are very small. So you can approximate with a drop or a pinch instead, keeping roughly the same proportions.

Rosemary Skin Lotion

This lotion contains ursolic acid, which expensive products use to combat wrinkles.

1. Put 3½–4 ounces (100–150 ml) of rubbing alcohol and a rosemary sprig in a plastic container, cover it tightly, and let it sit for two to three weeks. Shake it once every day. It will turn very dark green.
2. Pour ¼ ounce (6 ml) of this green liquid into a container with ⅛ ounce (3 ml) of glycerin and 4 ounces (120 ml) of distilled water and stir. Set in the refrigerator for one day.

Aloe Skin Lotion

This lotion is a moisturizer for people with dry skin.

1. Take a small- to medium-size leaf of an aloe plant. Cut off its prickly thorns and then cut the leaf up into 1-inch (about ½ cm) squares.
2. Put the squares and 1½ ounces (50 ml) of distilled water into a jar or plastic container.
3. Let it cool in the refrigerator for a couple days before using it.

Sake Lotion

This lotion is also a moisturizer. Apply it with a cotton pad and pat each area of the skin three times.

1. Mix 7 ounces (200 ml) of cold sake and 1½ pints (about 800 ml) of distilled water.
2. Put it in the refrigerator for a few days.

When you try out homemade lotions, apply them to your hands first to test them out. Make sure you have no allergic reaction before using them on other parts of your body or face. It's best to use up the lotion within two to three weeks.

VINEGAR AND WATER

When I visited my sister, I noticed she had a new morning routine: drinking vinegar in water.

According to her, vinegar and water makes her skin smooth and is good for digestion.

I told my high school friend about this. She said it is common in Japan nowadays, and she also does this. She doesn't like the vinegar taste so much, so she uses apple vinegar instead of rice vinegar.

How is this made? Just mix 1 part vinegar to 7 parts water.

6

green tea clean

INTRODUCTION

I have always thought that a big difference in cleaning methods between America and Japan is the sheer number and variety of cleaning liquids used here.

When I visited my mother-in-law, my sister-in-law, aunts, or friends in America, I saw their cabinets filled with rows of cleaning liquids, chemicals, and powders.

They had every kind of product for windows, floors, tile, toilet, stovetop and oven, stainless steel, carpets, furniture, computers, and so forth.

There was some "all new" or "improved" product for everything.

For a while, I enjoyed experimenting with a variety of cleaning liquids.

In my mother's house in Japan, there are no store-bought cleaning liquids.

She has *mottainai* (do not waste) spirit everywhere. She uses rice water to clean the hardwood floor, polishes the furniture with rice bran, washes windows with a wet cloth and newspaper, and sweeps the bathroom tiles with green tea leaves. (For more on the *mottainai* spirit, see pages 114–15.)

After a while, I went back to cleaning my mother's way, which I call Gentle Cleaning, here in America.

I love it. My hands don't get dried up, and there are no strong chemical smells in the house.

Using all natural substances gets the house just as clean, and I save money.

Not only that, all the household wastewater goes down into the sewer and may eventually flow into waterways. I feel much better because I'm contributing to a cleaner earth by not flushing potentially harmful chemicals down the drain.

In the long run, I think this is a conscientious and gentle way of treating the environment.

REPURPOSE EVERYDAY ITEMS FOR CLEANING SUPPLIES

rubber glove

toothbrush

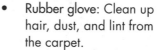

rubber band

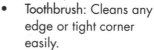

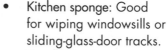

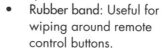

When cleaning day comes, it's important to have the appropriate cleaning materials in order to get as much cleaning done as you can.

Most people go out and buy cleaning supplies before starting the job. But if you look around the house you may find everyday items you can reuse for cleaning:

- Old cloth: Good for any kind of wiping and cleaning.
- Rubber glove: Clean up hair, dust, and lint from the carpet.
- Toothbrush: Cleans any edge or tight corner easily.
- Kitchen sponge: Good for wiping windowsills or sliding-glass-door tracks.
- Towel: Removes spiderwebs.
- Rubber band: Useful for wiping around remote control buttons.

EASY CARPET CARE

Carpet stains are easy to take care of with natural cleaning aids.

- Red wine: Before the wine soaks in, dab it with a dry cloth to take up as much of it as possible. Then put a little mountain of salt over it. The salt will absorb the wine. Later, just vacuum up the salt.
- Dark spots: Dab the spot with a hot, wet cloth and place a slice of lemon; the lemon has a bleaching effect.
- Gum: Put an ice cube on the gum wad for 1 to 2 minutes; after the gum hardens you can pick it off.
- Hairballs or dust bunnies: Put on a rubber glove and rub them. They come up very easily.
- Carpet dents: Heavy furniture makes dents in a carpet. Go over the dent with a steam iron and brush the carpet fibers to restore them.

BANANA PEELS

Next time you eat bananas, don't throw away the peels.

Banana peels can shine up your furniture, shoes, leather handbags—any kind of leather.

Clean away the dirt from the item with a cloth, and then rub it with the inside of a banana peel. Finally, buff it with a clean rag.

A banana peel has tannin, the same as leather, and like leather can bring out the shine in your shoes and bags.

Eat bananas and clean up your stuff. You are eating healthy and your things are bright and clean.

CLEAN SINKS AND TOILETS WITH VINEGAR

If you think your sink needs to be cleaned and shined, I recommend using vinegar. My orthodontist told me about routine cleaning for my retainer with white vinegar, so I fill a little cup with it and put my retainer in to soak. Every three days, I change the vinegar. (I have been doing this for fifteen years now.) When I pour the old vinegar in the sink, I notice how it brightens up the chrome ring around the drain.

Japanese people have been using vinegar for cleaning for a long time. Here are some suggestions:

- Clean the slime off the surface of the kitchen or bathroom sink.
- Clean and sanitize the cutting board. Mix 5 parts water to 1 part vinegar and spray it on the cutting board. This will kill bacteria.
- Remove soap scum from a bathtub with vinegar on a sponge.

- Use 3 parts water to 1 part vinegar to clean the floors. Soak a cloth with the solution and wipe your floor clean.

WAX FLOORS WITH GREEN TEA OR RICE WATER OR OLD MILK

For many years I used chemical cleaning liquids, but after I started research for this book, I switched to using only natural materials.

For example, try using some of the following liquids on your floors instead of wax and other commercial products; you'll be surprised how shiny they become! Sweep the floor first and then use a cloth, sponge, or mop to apply the "wax."

rice water

old milk

green tea

- Green tea: Reboil used green tea leaves. Remove the tea leaves with a strainer. Let the green water cool and add some fresh water.

- Rice water: This is the milky, white water that is produced when you wash and rinse your rice before cooking.
- Old milk: You can use milk after the expiration date on the carton.
- Boiled vegetable water: This is the water that remains after you boil certain vegetables like greens or potatoes.

CLEAN AND SHINE YOUR WINDOWS WITH SCRUNCHED-UP NEWSPAPERS

The best time for cleaning the windows is on a humid, cloudy day. The moisture in the air makes cleaning easier.

There are many commercial window-cleaning liquids to choose from, but from my experience, regular newspaper is best. You don't need chemicals.

Just dampen a sheet of newspaper, scrunch it up, and wipe the window in a circular motion. After that, scrunch up a dry newspaper and go over the window again to dry it off. And if you want a perfect finish, put salt on a wet cloth and clean around the window edges. You will be surprised at how shiny they become.

AN ACRYLIC SCRUBBING BRUSH

Have you ever heard of an acrylic scrubbing brush?

I was in a coffee shop in Tokyo, and next to my table were four middle-aged housewives who were touching small knitted things and talking about how wonderful they were. One of them had made the items and was giving them to the others

I couldn't figure out what they were.

It was a kitchen scrub brush! It was made of knitted acrylic fabric. My family in Japan uses these too.

This is an eco-friendly brush. You can use it for washing dishes or cleaning the sink, stove, or bathtub. The most important thing is, you don't need soap. You just wet it and scrub, and it gets things clean.

You are not using chemical substances so you are protecting the environment of your home, and you are using less water.

Because acrylic is made of very small fibers, it cleans very well. Use hot water. The fibers will cut through the dirt and grease, and the hot water will improve the disinfectant effect.

You can clean almost everything with it except very oily, dirty dishes. It is fine for lightly soiled dishes.

This scrub brush is sold in stores, but it is easy to knit. Use acrylic yarn from the yarn shop, or pulll out strands from an old sweater. The illustration shows a knitting pattern.

NATURAL AIR FRESHENER

You don't need to buy air freshener to get rid of odors in a room. There are natural substances to do the job. Here's how to deodorize the green way:

- Coffee: Place used coffee grounds, still in the paper filter, on a small tray and let them dry. Once they dry, staple the edges of the filter together at the top. You can use the dried coffee to deodorize shoes or to absorb odors in the refrigerator.
- Lemon: Cut up lemon peels into small pieces and put them on the bottom of the garbage can.
- Vinegar: Boil about 7 ounces (200 cc) of vinegar until it evaporates to freshen the air.
- Charcoal: Place pieces of charcoal around the house, anywhere you notice a foul smell. The charcoal will absorb the odors.
- Wet towel: Remove the smell of cigarettes by just taking a wet towel and wiping a fabric or surface up and down with it.
- Onions: Remove strong, fresh paint smells by cutting up an onion into eight sections and leaving them on a table in the room.

ONE TOWEL CLEANS EVERYTHING

Actually, you only need a single towel to do all your gentle cleaning.

You don't need extra storage space, and you don't need to spend money to buy commercial cleaning cloths.

Any time you want to clean, pick up the towel and begin.

Scrub, brush, wipe, and polish.

In the old days, people used only one cloth for cleaning.

If you spend 5 minutes every day to clean with a towel, your rooms can be virtually dirt free.

How easy.

corner

table top

spider web

PREVENT STEAMY MIRRORS—WITH POTATOES

Do your bathroom mirrors fog up while you are taking a hot shower? I always used a towel or Kleenex to clear up the mirrors, but I found out how to keep them from steaming up in the first place.

Peel a potato and rub a slice of it over the surface of the mirror. The potato is juicy and has starch granules that help absorb moisture.

When you get out of the shower, your face will be looking back at you in the mirror.

BAKING SODA CLEANING

Baking soda is cheap and effective for cleaning.

- Sprinkle it on a damp cloth to clean greasy surfaces.
- Make a paste of 3 parts baking soda to 1 part water. Rub the paste on silverware and then rinse with warm water.
- Add it to a litterbox to prevent odors.
- Sprinkle it on your wet dog and brush it out to remove that "wet dog" smell.
- Rinse old food jars with hot water and baking soda; if the smell remains, soak overnight.

7

eco-
laundry

INTRODUCTION

In America, I don't see clothes hanging outside to dry in the city.

Each time I go back to Tokyo, I see all kinds of clothes hanging in backyards or from balconies—undershirts, bikini underwear, bras, pantyhose, lingerie—all personal items. I notice this as I look out the window of the commuter train.

Skyscrapers, high-tech train systems, cell phones used as credit cards, smart homes with complicated computer systems—all these are part of daily life in Japan, but still people cling to many old-fashioned ways, including hanging their unmentionables outside for everyone to see.

Is this sex in the city on display?

Hanging laundry out has nothing to do with socio-economic class. Rich or poor, big house or tiny apartment, young or old, most people do it even if they do have a dryer.

Why? I guess people are more energy conscious or appreciative of the sun.

A lot of innovative ideas have come from the custom of hanging laundry out:

- quick-drying material for clothes, towels, sheets and socks
- lightweight, durable fabrics to withstand strong wind
- many different shapes and sizes of clothespins
- specially formulated laundry soap for people who work during the day, launder at night, and have to hang their clothes indoors while they sleep
- wrinkle-free clothes

If you have never hung your laundry outside, you might not feel comfortable doing it at first.

But just go ahead on a nice sunny day. Hang out some heavy things like jeans or big bath towels. It's something to feel good about. Stick with it for a month or two and look at how much you save on your gas or electric bill.

A small step will lead you to big savings on energy.

SIX WAYS TO HAND WASH

If you want to keep nice clothes looking good for a long time, you had better learn to hand wash.

Hand washing doesn't damage clothes.

My grandmother taught me six ways to hand wash in water.

1. *Oshi* wash: Press your hands down on the clothing item and push on it repeatedly. This forces the dirt out of the clothes.
2. *Tsukami* wash: Grab both sides of the cloth and squeeze it together.
3. *Momi* wash: Rub the cloth up and down on the side of your hand just below the thumb.
4. *Kosuri* wash: For shirt collars or socks, rub cloth on cloth.
5. *Tataki* wash: For delicate materials, lay the cloth on the palm of your hand, then

gently pat it with your other hand.

6. *Furi* wash: For silk, fold the cloth in half, grasp it tightly with your finger tips, and swish it up and down, then left and right.

SMELLY SOCKS

When you empty your clothes hamper, you will likely find smelly socks.

Soak the smelly socks in ½ cup vinegar and some water for about 30 minutes, then wash them with baking soda and detergent.

If you want to whiten socks, soak them in hot water with the juice of half a lemon.

Even heavy athletic socks will smell good and look bright and white.

In order not to lose matching pairs, pin the socks together with big safety pins.

REMOVE SWEATER PILLS

Even a nice sweater, if worn and cleaned many times, may get covered with many fuzz balls, especially if you wash it in the washing machine

You can do a couple things to prevent pills from forming or to remove them if they do form:

- Wash the sweater inside out.
- Rub masking tape over the sweater and snip the little balls with scissors.
- Stroke the sweater with the rough side of a dry kitchen sponge. I tried it, and the result was amazing! This is so easy and quick. Your sweater will look new again.

BLEACHING YELLOWY WHITES NATURALLY

If your white cotton fabrics have turned yellowish, you can use lemon to whiten them.

Put the item in hot water and squeeze the juice of one fresh lemon into the water. Leave the cloth overnight to soak.

In the morning the yellow will be gone.

THE BASICS

Do you know how to prepare your clothes for loading into the washing machine?

1. Separate whites and colors. Wash underwear with sheets and towels.
2. Put delicate clothes (bras, blouses, silks, and so forth) into a net bag.
3. First fill the machine with water, next add soap, and then the clothes. This order is important. The soap dissolves and your clothes wash evenly.

4. The heaviest or dirtiest clothes should be put on the bottom of the washing machine where there's more water pressure.
5. To prevent wrinkles, dry the clothes a shorter time, then remove and hang them up while they are still slightly damp.

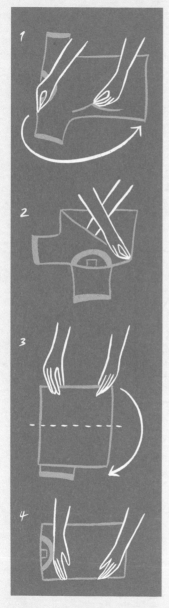

HOW TO FOLD CLOTHES

Has anyone ever taught you how to fold clothes?

Nobody taught me, I just did it my way.

One day my friend sent me an e-mail from Japan. She told me to take a look at a special way of folding. She said you can save 50% of your time when doing the laundry, and the clothes don't wrinkle. They keep their shape perfectly!

I tried it and I like it. It's a great hint.

You can use this technique for long-sleeve shirts, T-shirts, and sweaters

There are several YouTube videos that demonstrate this technique.

Here's one:

www.youtube.com/watch?v=dNr1oLhZ0zs&feature=related

HOW TO WASH CURTAINS

You don't need to send all your curtains to the dry cleaners. If you know how to handle the job, you can do it at home.

- Thin, white curtains: Use ½ cup of laundry soap and ½ cup of baking soda and wash them on the delicate cycle.
- Heavy curtains: Spot clean only. Mix 1 part baking soda and 1 part water to make a paste. Apply the paste to the dirty spot and leave it there while it dries. Then brush it off (the paste absorbs dirt).

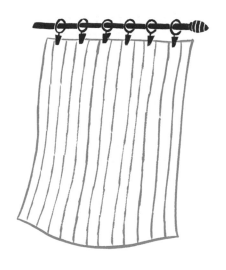

- White lace curtains: Fill the washtub about halfway; add ½ cup of vinegar and 3 tablespoons of salt. Put in the curtains and soak them for 1 hour, then rinse. Finally, wash them with laundry soap on the delicate cycle. Do not use the dryer to dry the curtains. Hang them back up on the curtain rods. They will dry nicely and won't wrinkle. It looks like a professional job.

PREVENT COLORS FROM FADING

Have you ever washed colored clothes and whites together?

When you took out the clothes from the washer, maybe you found a pink or bluish shirt or blouse that used to be white.

You thought you couldn't wear it anymore.

There is a way to wash some colors and whites together. Before washing the colors for the first time, check the label to see if the color might fade.

Add 3 tablespoons of salt along with the laundry soap into the water in the machine.

The salt will prevent colors from fading.

VINEGAR FOR FABRIC SOFTENER

Do you use softener for your laundry?

It is a good idea to soften your fabrics, especially if you have kids or if someone in the family is sick.

The commercial softeners you buy at the store may not be that good. They are not natural and they include chemicals.

Let's use an organic item: vinegar.

During the rinse cycle, add 3 tablespoons of vinegar to the water.

Your clothes will come out nice and soft, and there will be no smell of the vinegar.

You will love it!

HANG YOUR CLOTHES OUTSIDE WITH CLOTHESPINS

If you want to save on your electric and gas bill, try hanging your laundry outside.

In Japan we have a very handy laundry hanger designed to hang from a line or laundry pole. It is compact and easy to carry inside and outside. It is square or round with lots of clothespin-like like clips attached, and usually, you can get twenty to thirty pieces of laundry on it. If a couple needs just one, a family needs two.

It's also easy to use a clothesline and wire hangers from the dry cleaner.

Here are some tips on how to hang laundry out to dry:

- On a bright, sunny day, turn your clothes inside out in order to avoid fading.
- Clip a pair of socks together at the top with a laundry pin, then hang them over the bottom of a plastic hanger hanging from the clothesline.
- Hang T-shirts on a wire hanger on the

clothesline. They will dry faster and wrinkle less.

- Clip the top of a skirt on a round laundry hanger using several pins. The air will blow through and dry it quickly.
- Hang sheets over the clothesline in the shape of a triangle. The water in the fabric drips down to the point of the triangle and the sheets dry faster.

SORT CLOTHES QUICKLY

Here's the best way to eliminate time spent sorting clothes.

First, use big laundry pins to fasten net laundry bags to the household hamper or laundry basket.

Each net bag will be for a different type of item: socks, underwear, delicates, colors. Tell everyone in the family which bag is for what.

When it's time to do the wash, zip up each bag and toss it in the washing machine. You will never need to hunt for missing socks again.

Net laundry bags come in small, medium, and large sizes, so you can wash almost anything in them.

8

recycling and reusing

INTRODUCTION

All the world has started to rethink how to use our planet's limited energy resources.

In Japan, you can hear and see the word *sai*. This word is everywhere. It means recycle and reuse.

People everywhere are more concerned about the environment than ever before.

Grandma said, and my mother, and other elderly people are saying, *mottainai*.

Even I use this word so often. The expressions closest to *mottainai* in English are "what a waste," "do not waste," or "used without good care and consideration."

Now this word *mottainai* has become an eco-word given by Japan to the world.

Kenyan environmentalist Wngri Maathai, who was awarded the Nobel Peace Prize in 2004, has promoted the concept of *mottainai* as a term that is equivalent to the English phrase "reduce, reuse, recycle."

My mother is a super *mottainai* person. She still has clothes from my father and my late grandmother, and even from me when I was young.

From these old clothes she makes mop slippers. What she does is cut out squares of cotton cloth, layer them on top of each other, and sew them up on three sides. One side is left open so she can slide her feet in. She is getting old, so it's hard for her to bend and wipe the floor, but she can put on her mop slippers and slowly walk around to clean the hardwood, tatami, or vinyl floors.

Mottainai helps you think about not wasting and about using things again.

In everyday life we use dozens of things and then just throw them away, or maybe we let other things just sit in a closet or in the garage for months or years.

Perhaps we need to rethink what to do with all this stuff. Can we use it? Maybe you can find your own things to recycle and reuse.

WIRE HANGERS

We often get wire hangers from the dry cleaners. We can reuse these in many ways:

- After washing sneakers: Grab both ends of a wire hanger and bend them up. Then you can hang wet sneakers or slippers over the ends to dry

sneakers

- To freshen your pillows: Get two hangers. Pull down on each hanger from the middle point of the bottom, and spread it out. You'll get two diamond-shaped hangers. Hang the hangers about fourteen inches apart and support the ends of the pillow by placing them through the hangers' openings.
- For your trousers: Take a cardboard aluminum foil or saran wrap roller and cut it the entire length of one side. Slip the

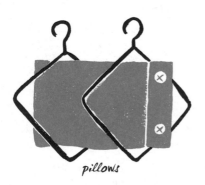

pillows

cardboard over the bottom of the hanger, then hang your pants over the roller to prevent wrinkles and creases across the legs.

- For baby clothes: This turns a large hanger into a small one. Take a needle-nose pliers and grip the middle of the curved end of the hanger from the inside, then pull it toward the center. Repeat on the other side. The hanger will have two sideways Vs on each end.

kids clothing

- Drying jeans: On a nice day, here's how to hang your jeans outside. Clip two hangers together at the top. Then bend the hangers slightly away from each other. Hang the jeans so they rest on the ends of the hangers. The air flows through evenly and the jeans are not likely to shrink.
- Wet cap or light raincoat: Bend up each end of a hanger to make a 90-degree angle. Put the hanger on a hook in your garage or by your back door. This makes an easy place to hang wet outerwear on a rainy day.

ALUMINUM FOIL

If you have leftover fried chicken from yesterday, how do you warm it up?

Put it in the microwave? Yes, that's an easy way, but the chicken won't get crispy. It will get oily, soft, and soggy.

Everyone has leftover food. Next time you use foil for reheating, don't throw it away. Usually, foil can be used twice (if it's not too greasy), so keep it in the toaster oven to use again.

Just wrap up fried food in the foil and reheat it in the toaster oven. It will be less oily and more crispy.

sharpen
scissors

Here's another way to reuse foil:

Foil is good for sharpening knives or scissors in a flash. Just cut into three layers of foil eight to ten times with a knife or scissors, and the metallic foil will give your dull blades a new edge.

Or, scrunch up some aluminum foil into a ball. Use the ball to scrub and scrape around the edges of a stovetops's gas burner to remove grease and grime (don't scratch the smooth porcelain-like surface of the stove, however!). You'll hardly need any energy at all.

How simple and useful!

ORGANIC DYE: CHANGING THE COLOR OF FABRIC

If you get tired of the color of some fabrics or clothes, or if old whites look dingy or drab—and you still like the style—there is an easy solution. You can change the color! You will be surprised how this can brighten up old clothes or fabrics.

You could, of course, buy a commercial dye, but you can use things from the kitchen or flowers from your eco-friendly garden.

- Dark brown: Coffee
- Reddish brown: English tea
- Yellow: Saffron
- Pink: Cherry blossom flowers, roses
- Purple: Red onion skins
- Light brown or yellow: Cinnamon
- Light blue: Gardenias
- Light green: *Matcha* (green tea powder)

Here's how to use these eco-friendly colors:

1. Boil the dye substance in water on low heat for about 1 hour.
2. Put the cloth in the dye pot at the same low heat for 15 to 30 minutes.
3. Stir frequently in order to avoid uneven coloring.
4. Check to make sure the color is even and rinse the cloth well.

5. After rinsing, put the cloth in a bowl with *myoban* (a type of alum, used to fix the dye) and soak 15 to 20 minutes.
6. Rinse the cloth again and hang it outside in the shade.

PLASTIC BOTTLES

toilet roll

cat food

Plastic bottles, especially water bottles and 1-liter soda bottles, are everywhere, and it's wasteful to just use them once and toss them away. There are many things you can do with a plastic bottle.

- In an earlier chapter, I talked about the *yutanpo* (hot water bottle for keeping your feet warm). If you can't find one, make your own (it makes a good foot-warmer!). Put hot water into a plastic bottle and tighten the cap firmly. Wrap it well with a towel. In cold weather, you can put it next to your cold feet, stomach, legs, or any part of your body that you want to warm up while you sleep. It will keep you warm until morning, and you can sleep well. After using the bottle, you can recycle it. Give the water to your plants first.

- Cut a regular-size plastic bottle in half. Hold the top part upside down. You can use it as a funnel. For example, use it to transfer tablets or pills from one container to another.

- Use this idea for keeping toilet paper in your car. Cut off the flat bottom of a plastic bottle. Put a half-used roll of toilet paper in it. Run a strand of paper up through the hole and pull out as needed. You'll avoid taking too much at once, and the paper won't gather dust.

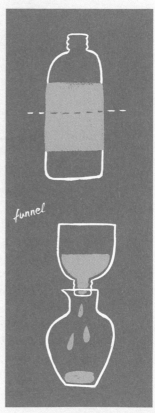

funnel

- Cut a clear plastic bottle in half to use the bottom part as a planter for seedlings. Put soil in it and plant a vegetable or flower. Hang it up with wire. You can see the condition of the soil inside to tell if it is dry or wet.

- Use water-filled bottles as weights when you exercise. Hold the bottles as you run or walk. If you get thirsty, you can drink the water.

- Put frozen corn or mixed veggies in a clear plastic Gatorade bottle.

It is easy to see how much is left, and the standing bottles are easy to organize. This works better than piling bags on top of each other.

- Use a big, clear plastic bottle for keeping rice. You can see inside, and the cap keeps out bugs.
- Keep dry cat food in any size plastic bottle. It's easier to pour into the kitty's dish than lifting and pouring from a big, heavy bag.

ECO-GARDENING

Would you like to grow organic vegetables?

There are some safe, easy, eco-friendly ways to do it while avoiding the use of chemicals.

After drinking black tea, green tea, or coffee, don't throw away the leaves or grounds.

You can use them in planters or in the ground to fertilize your flowers, vegetables, or green plants. Just sprinkle the leaves or grounds around the plants and watch them grow colorful and strong.

Also, you can use cooled water left over from boiling vegetables or eggs to water plants. The nutrients from the veggies or eggs enrich the soil and feed the plants.

And don't forget that eggshells are good for plants, too. Crush them up and spread them on top of the soil.

How about getting rid of insects or pests while you are at it?

- Slugs: Try putting salt on them. They dissolve. Don't put salt near the plants because it kills them.
- Aphids: Spray or splash milk on the leaves.
- Ants: Drench with soapy water.

ORANGE PEELS

Next time you eat an orange, don't throw away the peel. You can use it. You'll be surprised how versatile it is:

- Moisten a peel with water to wipe oily, dirty dishes. They will be clean and shiny.
- After cleaning up the dishes, use orange peels for cleaning the sink and faucet; the pectin acts as a coating for the sink.
- Polish furniture with it.
- Wrap it in gauze and put it in bathwater. Vitamins C and A moisten and soothe your skin.
- Dice it into small, thin pieces for orange marmalade.
- Make potpourri: Place orange peelings on an open newspaper and let them dry until they turn hard. Then put them in a cotton bag and

hang it in the room. Odors will disappear.

- Clean the tatami or bamboo mat: Boil orange peels for about 15 minutes. Dampen a cloth with the boiled water and wipe the tatami or bamboo mat until it's clean and fresh.
- Place some dried orange peels in the microwave and cook them for 1 minute. The inside of the microwave will smell fresh.
- Boil dried orange peels for 15 minutes. After that you can use the boiled water as a glass cleaner.
- When fish or garbage leaves an unpleasant scent in the kitchen, just cut up some dried orange peels and place them in a dish on the countertop. The odors will vanish and a fresh smell remains.

RECYCLING AND REUSING CARDBOARD ROLLERS

Foil or plastic wrap has a rigid cardboard roller inside. After the wrap or foil is gone, you can get extra use out of the roller:

- Sprinkle flour on cookie dough and use it as a rolling pin.
- Press the open end down on the cookie dough to make a round cut.
- Roll up leftover pieces or scraps of wrapping

paper or gift wrap that you don't want to throw way, then tighten it onto the roller with a rubber band. If your leftovers are too long, tape two rollers together.

hold gift wrap

save diplomas and awards

- To save your kids' printed certificates of achievement, or if anyone in the family has received awards, roll them up tightly and put them around or inside the tube to keep them from getting wrinkled or torn before or after you put them up on the wall.

DISPOSABLE CHOPSTICKS

Disposable chopsticks are made of wood. If you go to an Asian supermarket and buy ready-to-eat items, you will get disposable chopsticks. You often get them at Asian restaurants, too.

But so many are just tossed away! A Japanese paper company reports that 6 recycled disposable chopsticks are enough to make one sheet of copy paper. Two hundred chopsticks can produce one weekly magazine, while 300 chopsticks can be transformed into 500 facial tissues!

There are lots of ways to reuse chopsticks. Here are a couple ideas from Japan:

- Toothpaste push-up: Cut two sticks in half and place each half across the bottom of an almost used-up tube of toothpaste. Tie the ends of the sticks together with a rubber band, then roll up the tube over the sticks. You can get the very last dab of toothpaste from the tube.
- Toilet cleaner: Small nooks and crannies on a toilet are hard to clean. Wrap a small piece of old cloth over the end of a chopstick and attach it with a rubber band. Spray toilet cleaner on it, then clean those little curves and corners.
- Flower label: After planting seeds, poke a chopstick up through the seed packet and gently push the end through the paper. Then push the bottom of the stick into the soil. You have a visual reminder of what you have planted.

USE COFFEE GROUNDS TO BE GREEN

Many people drink coffee at home and at work all day long.

My friend Melanie bags up the leftover grounds and takes them home.

I was wondering what she was going to use them for. She said, "It's for compost!" She is soooo greeeeen!

Here are a few ways you can use coffee grounds:

- For compost.
- To put right in the garden soil for fertilizer.
- As a bug deterrent: Ants don't like coffee, so they won't cross a line of coffee grounds.
- To soak up oil from pots and pans: Leftover cooking oil on the frying pan is thick—you don't want it to go down the drain; coffee grounds absorb the oil, so it is easy to get the pan clean while using less soap.
- To clean off an oily plastic container: Rub the container with coffee grounds and the sticky oil will be gone.

OLD CLOTHES

Each year new fashions appear, and even if we don't need them, we buy them anyway.

We enjoy new colors and designs. But how about our old clothes? If you buy new ones, you have to make space for them. Otherwise, you can't get the closet door closed.

I started to exchange clothes with friends. Twice a year we bring old or new or never-worn clothes to each other's homes. Each of us picks some clothes that fit. If there are leftovers that nobody wants, we donate them to charity.

Therefore, for the past few years, I have hardly ever needed to buy any new clothes. I always find something I like among my friends' "discards."

One of my friends is much younger than I am, so she buys trendy new things every year. This puts me one season behind the latest fashion, but I don't have to go to an office every day, so it doesn't really matter. I enjoy the different styles, and after I've worn them for awhile, I drop them off at Goodwill or the Salvation Army.

My husband wears my son's old T-shirts or sweaters or sweatshirts from last season, so he can enjoy the trendy looks, too.

After the T-shirts or sweatshirts get old, I use them to cover up my shoulders and neck when I dye my hair. I also wear them for pajamas or for doing yard work or heavy cleaning.

And then, when they get worn really thin, I cut them up into small pieces and use them for bath and toilet cleaning. Finally, I throw them away.

Old socks are good for cleaning light bulbs, and old bath towels can be turned into bath mats. You can make them kid's size or big size. And they are so easy to wash and dry.

Old clothes and towels can be used for years and years.

MAGAZINE AND CALENDAR PAPER

It was my birthday. I got a present with beautiful wrapping paper picturing a cat. It was from my friend who loved animals.

She had used calendar paper to wrap the gift. She knew I liked cats, so the wrapping looked so cute to me, and I felt she had given my gift special attention.

When my mother sends me something from Japan to America, she always wraps it in Japanese newspaper. Because I don't get the daily newspaper from Tokyo, the news is actually a couple weeks old, but the advertising or local updates refresh my memory of life in my hometown

If you look around the house, you can find all kinds of paper for wrapping.

Magazines nowadays have beautiful color pages bursting with art or photography. Use them to to make gift cards and envelopes, as well as wrapping paper.

A foreign-language newspaper is a nice touch for wrapping a present from a short trip abroad, and it protects the gift, too.

Magazine covers and calendar paper are a good choice for book covers because the paper is heavier and tear resistant.

OLD PHONE BOOK

Every year we get a new phone book.

When you get one this year, don't throw the old one away. You can use it to protect floors or shelves.

In your kitchen cabinets or garage set drippy or oily containers on top of an old phone book to avoid stains and messes. I use one under a vegetable oil container or olive oil bottle.

After the top layer of paper gets wet or oily, I just rip out some pages from the book, throw them away, and start again with a clean surface.

EGG CARTONS

When I visit my aunt's house in the winter, I notice green plants sprouting up inside egg cartons sitting on her kitchen counter. This little patch of green makes the cold winter feel like a warm spring.

We get egg cartons every time we buy eggs. Are there any good ideas for reusing them?

Here are a few:

- Use them as a place to germinate flower seeds or saplings before you are ready to put them in flower pots or in the ground.
- Turn them into jewlery boxes to keep earrings, bracelets, necklaces, or rings.
- Let them hold dabs of paint for artwork or for touch ups on trim or other surfaces.

And they're great for storing golf balls!

9

green tea zone

INTRODUCTION

Going green is not just done at home. It is even more important in public places.

Somehow, people think they may not be responsible for what they do outside their homes.

According to *The Green Book* by Elizabeth Rogers and Thomas M. Kostigen, the average U.S. office worker uses 10,000 sheets of copy paper each year. The annual total is 21 million tons of copy paper, or more than 4 trillion sheets. That's a huge amount of paper and accounts for cutting more and more trees, so workers in many offices try to reduce waste by using both sides of the paper or writing memos on discarded sheets.

In Japan, the government started energy-saving programs called "coolbiz" and "warmbiz" to cut costs for air conditioning and heating in office buildings. Men wear no ties or jackets in summer, and the thermostat is set at 82°F (28°C). In winter, people wear warmer clothes and the temperature is 68–72°F (20–22°C). During the past four years, people have gotten used to the practice and are cooperating.

For shopping, people carry the eco-bag. This is really a re-creation of the *furoshiki* that is hundreds of years old: a simple square or rectangular cloth that can be folded and tied in many ways to carry, wrap, or protect items like gifts, lunches, books, and so on. This traditional item has been given new and modern designs, and Japanese young people think it's fashionable, so what's old is new again.

Something as simple as carrying a handkerchief with you when you go out is a way to use fewer paper products like napkins, tissues, or paper towels. Taking your own things from home when you go to work, school, or on a trip is an easy yet effective way to help save resources.

CARRY A *FUROSHIKI* (ECO-BAG)

The *furoshiki* wrapping/carrying cloth is a wonderful idea for living sustainably.

The *furoshiki* is a type of traditional Japanese wrapping cloth that was often used to carry clothes, gifts, or other goods. It is rectangular in shape and in size is commonly (and approximately) 17 inches (45 cm) by 26–28 inches (68–72 cm).

People started using the *furoshiki* in the Edo period (1603–1868). They carried it to the public bath, wrapping up their towels, soap, and clothes inside it. It was easy to carry these loose items by wrapping them up together in a cloth. (By the way, *furo* means "bath.")

Also during the Edo period, fires often broke out in the towns. Citizens could use the *furoshiki* for packing up personal belongings and having it ready in case of an emergency evacuation. They always prepared a *furoshiki* before sleep, and history tellls us they kept it under their futon (mattress), just in case.

The *furoshiki* was perfect for wrapping both big and small things. Unfortunately, plastic shopping bags took the place of the *furoshiki* over the decades.

In recent years, there has been a renewed interest in the *furoshiki* because it's reusable.

So now, in the modern world, it is very popular again. The new *furoshiki* are made of silk, cotton, rayon, or *chirimen* (crepe). There are both traditional and contemporary designs. Young people are wearing *furoshiki* as scarves, too.

On the opposite and following pages are a few common *furoshiki* folding methods.

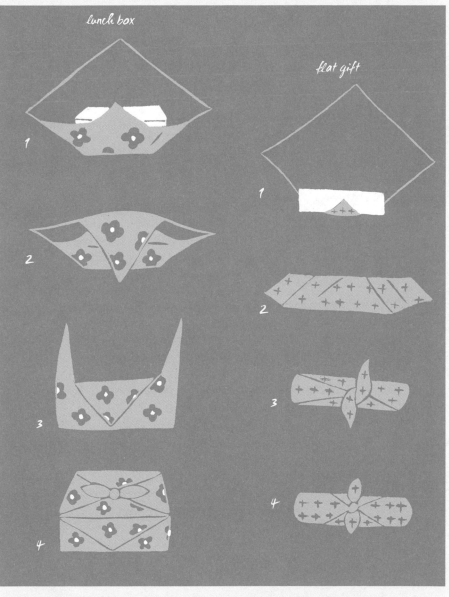

lunch box

flat gift

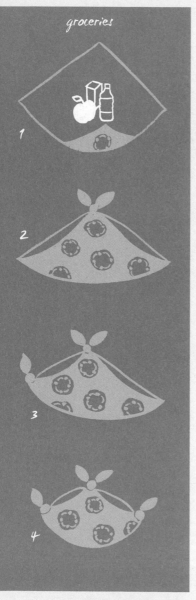

groceries

1

2

3

4

BRING A LUNCH BOX TO WORK OR SCHOOL

If you are concerned about your weight and health, I recommend that you take a lunch box with you. Carrying a lunch box is going green!

School lunch in America is totally different from that in Japan. American parents pack a sandwich, an apple or some other fruit, and packaged snacks in a brown bag, so kids can throw it away when they're finished.

Japanese kids carry a *bento* box in a wrapping cloth *(furoshiki)* to school. The wrapping cloth can be used as a place mat. Inside the *bento* box are usually foods of five different colors: white for rice, noodles, or bread (carbo-hydrates); green for vegetables (vita-mins); yellow for a fried or boiled egg (lipids); red for a sour plum (minerals); and brown for the fish or meat (protein). The color coordination means a bal-anced diet, and the lunch box is not something to be thrown away. It is kept and reused every day for a long time.

From this daily practice, kids learn about a balanced diet and not to waste.

Taking a lunch box can save you a

lot of money, too. If you usually spend $15 including a drink at a restaurant every day, monthly you spend over $330. Yearly, that's about $4,000. This is big money for lunch. If you have high blood pressure or high cholesterol, it's very hard to monitor the ingredients of a restaurant order. Carrying

your own lunch box and managing what and how much you put in it is better for your health and your budget.

WASH YOUR HANDS WITH AN *OSHIBORI* BEFORE EATING

An *oshibori* is a small, rolled-up, wet hand towel. The *oshibori* is used for cleaning the hands before eating.

We touch a lot of things throughout the day, but we don't always get a chance to go to the restroom to wash up before eating.

So bacteria or viruses might be sticking to our hands. By using an *oshibori*, you can save water and avoid using paper towels and still sanitize your hands. Not only that, you will be less exposed to bacteria by decreasing the number of times you visit a public restroom.

The Japanese use chopsticks most of the time when they

eat. Even so, they are very careful about keeping their hands clean.

In America we eat burgers and fries, sandwiches, chips, appetizers, fried chicken, pizza, and fruit with our fingers, but we don't always get the chance to wash our hands. The *oshibori* is usually offered at restaurants, but nowadays most airlines offer them to passengers before a meal service. Even American and European carriers are handing them out as a courtesy. The *oshibori* is not only for restaurants and the travel industry. When Japanese people go on a picnic or to the beach, they take their own *oshibori*.

There are two kinds of *oshibori*. Cold *oshibori* are used in summer, and hot *oshibori* in winter.

You can use a wet face towel and put it in a plastic bag inside your briefcase, backpack, or school bag. It is really convenient for your daily activities.

CARRY A THERMOS

When I was young I always carried a thermos out with me to public places. In those days we didn't have plastic water bottles. You had to carry drinks in a thermos.

On school trips or for special events or afternoon activities, we brought our own drinks.

It was convenient to have a thermos, but in recent years, we've learned to think of convenience differently. Our habits have changed. Just buy a drink in a plastic bottle when you get thirsty rather than carry the thermos with you from home.

When you are done, throw it away.

Well, now look what's happening. People have started to get concerned with protecting the environment.

Working people and schoolkids are carrying their own cups and thermos bottles to job sites and school for sensible, economical reasons.

If you buy a bottled drink every day for a month at $1.50 per bottle, it costs $45.

And, if you use a thermos, you don't need to worry about toxic chemical pollution from the highly reactive plastic molecules in the "convenience" bottles. For that matter, you don't have to worry about being poisoned by them.

Any way you look at it, a thermos is environmentally friendly and protective of your health.

It's kind of fun choosing your own thermos. They come in all different materials, colors, and sizes.

So be sure to always carry your thermos with you. You can fill it at any time with hot or cold water. Take green or herbal or black tea bags or drip coffee packets with you too, so you can enjoy a variety of tastes anywhere you go.

USE A HANDKERCHIEF

Do you have a handkerchief? Before sending her family off to work or school, a Japanese mom always asks this. It has been a custom in Japan for a long time. The Japanese did not have paper towels or hot air blowers in public restrooms in years past, so the handkerchief was a necessity for going out to public places. That said, there are many ways you can go green with a handkerchief.

How else do the Japanese use a handkerchief? Here are some of the ways:

- Wrap up a small gift in a handkerchief.
- Wipe the sweat away from your face or arms on sticky, summer days.
- When you spill sauce or ketchup and make a stain, you can wet a handkerchief with water or soap and clean up the mess immediately.
- Wipe a runny nose.
- Wrap it around your neck on a cold or windy day.
- If you get an injury on the arm, leg, or foot, you can use it for first aid: clean up, tie it up, and stop the bleeding.
- Wear it as a headband to absorb sweat from your brow.
- When a chair or floor is dirty, you can cover it and sit down.
- Use it as a napkin for lunch at your desk or on a bench.
- Put it in the pocket of a formal suit jacket.

small gift

neck warmer

stain remover

bandage

dress up

WRITE MEMOS OR NOTES ON USED PRINTER PAPER

Here is a simple way to stop wasting paper for business or school.

We use tons of paper for computer or fax printers.

I went to the famous Kikumaru Beauty Salon in the Ginza in Tokyo. The owner is very well known in the media, so high-fashion models or famous people go there to have their hair styled.

I noticed the scratch paper next to the phone and on his office desk. It was all used printer paper.

I felt curious about this. In this shop, people paid over $150 for a haircut. The owner gave expert advice and suggestions about hairstyles, shampoo, conditioners, and fashion coordination. Yet instead of using fancy memo paper, he would cut up squares from old ads (printed on one side) or printer paper.

He reminded me of Grandma. She was always cutting up old ads or calendar paper for memos.

I asked him, "Why?" Dumb question!

He said, "If each one is careful about using paper, it will eventually make a big difference in the future for saving trees. When you are done with the memo, you put it in the recycle bin."

He is very concerned about going green.

COOL OFF WITH A PAPER FAN

People have forgotten many useful ideas from the old days.

A handheld fan (*sensu* or *uchiwa*) is used for cooling or refreshing oneself. A paper hand fan waved back and forth creates airflow.

When it is very hot, you move it quickly back and forth; the fan provides cooling by increasing the airflow over the skin, which in turn increases the evaporation of sweat droplets on the skin. This evaporation has a cooling effect.

A hand fan is shaped like a half circle. Its thin material is mounted on slats that can be folded and closed when not in use, so it's very compact. You can put it in your bag or backpack and take it anywhere you go.

Use it on public transportation, at the office, at school or anywhere you cannot control air temperature. You get relief from the heat even when others around you don't.

It is very simple and there is no cost for electricity.

You can get cool air you can control by yourself.

What a simple idea!

WEAR TOE SOCKS

People wear socks inside of tight shoes for many long hours at a time at work and school.

When I saw my son wearing five-toe socks for going to work in Japan, I became curious. I hadn't seen such socks before, but I learned that they became very popular in Japan after a Japanese company started to sell them in 1981.

Five-toe socks are good for you for several reasons:

- Five-toe socks help support your whole body evenly; therefore, you can stand up straight and strong. They are good for sports and blue-collar work.
- If the five toes of your feet are free to move, you have good blood circulation, which also stimulates the brain.
- With your five toes grabbing the floor, your posture improves.
- Each toe is covered by a cozy fabric. As your toes and feet warm up, your whole body does, too.

- There is a pressure point between toes two and three that is linked to the stomach, so stimulating that area is good for digestion.
- You don't get athlete's foot—there is no fungal growth between the toes.

Even MLB players Hideki Matsui and Hideki Okajima wear five-toe socks.

PRACTICE "COOLBIZ" AND "WARMBIZ" AT THE OFFICE

In the summer of 2005, the "coolbiz" campaign was proposed by then–Prime Minister Koizumi. This was an effort to help reduce consumption of electricity in the workplace by limiting the use of air conditioning. Thermostats were set at 82°F (28°C) until September. Prime Minister Koizumi started to wear short-sleeved shirts without jackets or ties. The coolbiz dress code advises workers to starch collars so they stand up loosely and to wear trousers made from materials that breathe. Many government workers said they felt improper or impolite not wearing a tie when meeting counterparts from the private sector.

Could government bureaucrats go without ties and jackets? A couple years later, everybody was dressed for coolbiz. They felt less sweaty and fatigued from the heat, and learned to feel properly comfortable for doing business without the jackets and ties.

Also, in the winter of 2005, the major news networks began promoting a "warmbiz" style for winter. Office temperatures were set at 68°–72°F (20°–22°C). This can feel kind of cold for an office. It was suggested that people wear heavy turtleneck shirts instead of collared shirts and a tie. Warmbiz was not endorsed by the Japanese government, but people began to wear warmer clothes at the office to help save energy.

So, if adapting your style of clothing helps to save energy, it just naturally contributes to saving our precious resources—oil, natural gas, and coal. This is an idea for all the world. British trade unions and the U.S. Congress have promoted their own coolbiz campaigns since the summer of 2006.

ADOPT THE "MY HASHI" RULE

Take your own *hashi* (chopsticks) to a restaurant, work, school, or on a trip. For an American option, take your own silverware.

The "My Hashi" (chopstick) movement has been taking place in Japan for several years now. People use disposable *hashi* (or *waribashi*, natural wood chopsticks you pull apart) at the rate of about 250 million a year.

A single Japanese uses 200 disposable chopsticks a year. If each of us can carry our own reusable *hashi*, we can save lots of trees.

This is one small example of how to save our forests. This is not hard to do. It's actually fun. You can find your own attractive cloth chopstick case with a nice color and unique design that's made of good fabric.

Carrying a "My Hashi" case is really quite trendy.

For those who prefer to use a fork, go ahead and do that. It's actually safer to carry your own, since at least you know your own silverware is clean.

Or if you want to experience Asian cuisine, just take your own *hashi* to a Chinese or Japanese restaurant. In the long run, you and conscientious others will be helping to preserve a precious natural resource, our forests.

10

economic zen

INTRODUCTION

I was watching the news about the Black Friday sales after Thanksgiving in 2008.

The news reporter said, "This year, because of the recession, some retail sales are down by as much as 25%, but many Asian families in America may be spending more than other families. Why? Because they have a different approach to saving money."

I thought this comment was very interesting.

According to the Organisation for Economic Co-operation and Development, in 2007 the average American household kept 12.9% of their savings in cash and 30.4% in stock. Japanese keep 50.1% of their savings in cash and 12.2% in stock.

You can tell from this report that stockholders were vulnerable to losing a big part of their assets in the financial crisis of 2008. People with insured cash savings are in a stronger position to withstand the effects of a bad economy.

A bad economy also teaches hard lessons about having too much debt.

Nobody really wants to be controlled by money and debt. It feels much better to be in control of your money.

It might be time to create a budget. A budget allows you to understand where money goes and may help you free up cash for savings.

Green tea saving and spending ideas might help you pay off debt and gain strength to get through financial crises.

SPEND CASH WHEN YOU HAVE IT— DON'T USE CREDIT

After I moved to America, I noticed a big difference between the way Japanese and Americans use money.

It seems to me Americans don't have much cash in their wallets—even less than $10. I often saw people buying fast food with credit cards.

Japanese people carry at least $100 to $200 in their wallets. They pay cash at restaurants, the grocery store, and movies. Usually, anything that costs less than $100 is paid for in cash.

- There are benefits to paying cash.
- You can control cash. It's simple. You take a look in your wallet, and you see how much you can spend.
- If you pay cash, you immediately recognize the value of the goods and services you are paying for.
- You avoid adding to your debt. If you don't have money, you don't use it.

Cash spending has limits,

but credit card spending may lead to reckless and unnecessary purchases. You can accumulate $5,000 on your credit card in a hurry.

CASH YOUR PAYCHECK AND DIVIDE IT UP

On payday, my mother would always go to the bank. She would take out almost all of the cash except what was designated for automatic bill payments.

At home she would count out the cash and put set amounts into several different envelopes—one each for education, food, utilities, insurance, newspaper subscriptions, and so forth.

After each amount of money was tucked into its envelope, she would figure out which leftover sums could be put into savings or used for entertainment.

Each month would be different depending on what family events were planned.

She did this from way back, ever since I was a baby, so she almost always managed to stay within her budget and not spend more than the income.

It was an easy way for my mother to see where the money went and to always remember to set aside some for saving.

We once had many rainy days, after my father lost his job, but with the savings, I did not even realize my father had been out of work. My mother told me about it years later after I had had my first baby.

She had an umbrella to protect us on those rainy days.

Now, I am trying it my own way. First, our paychecks go into the savings account by direct deposit. I transfer funds online to the checking account as they are needed for paying the bills. I just make sure to leave at least 10% in savings each month.

This is my modern way, but it's really doing the same thing electronically that my mother was doing for years and years with cash and envelopes.

$100 A MONTH PER PERSON FOR FOOD

How many ways are there to cut the household budget?

Utilities, water, phone . . . these expenses are hard to cut and the results don't amount to much, even if you try hard.

One thing you can really have control over is how much you decide to spend for food. If you have a family, you can aim for $100 per person monthly. (Of course this is just a rough number, and with prices going up you'll always have to make adjustments.)

If you make up your mind to spend less to feed the family, you will find out there are many ways to save money on food:

- Avoid going out to restaurants so often.
- Do not go shopping when you are hungry.
- Use up leftover food from the refrigerator once or twice a week.
- Eat more veggies than meat; they are cheaper

and healthier.
- Plan to use today's dinner's leftovers to prepare tomorrow's lunch.
- Keep your supermarket receipts and record how much you spend. If you're going over your budget of $100 per person per month, you'll be able to figure out what you are overspending on.

10% FOR PLAY MONEY

We need balance in our lives. That includes balancing out how much money you make and how much you spend. Think of the joy of spending money for yourself.

Play money is for you to use to relax, enjoy yourself, and reduce stress.

Happy money brings happiness.

When you enjoy money, you appreciate it and understand its value.

If you use 10% of your income for yourself, it's the same as saving 10%.

If you let money control you, you may be missing out on more satisfying reasons for living, but if you take control of your money you are more in charge of how to live.

If money isn't adding good to our lives, why are we working so hard?

10% FOR SAVING

A Japanese proverb says, in so many words, "Many a little makes a mickle."

Since I was a kid, I put a little money at a time in a piggy bank so that I was saving every month. This way of saving doesn't grow big soon, but if you are patient, you will be glad someday that you have it.

I saved money from age eight to eighteen. I put away some from my pocket money and from part-time jobs.

I put it in the bank in CDs. In those days interest was 7%. My mother, who managed a limited amount of money from my father's income, told me she thought this was a safe and easy way to make relatively little money grow bigger.

She taught me the Rule of 72. This is how to figure when your principal will be doubled: divide the number 72 by the interest rate. If the annual interest rate is 10%, divide it into 72 ($72 \div 10 = 7.2$). That means it takes 7.2 years for your principal to double. If the rate is 7%, ($72 \div 7 = 10.3$), then it takes 10.3 years.

When I was nineteen years old, I went abroad for the first time. I visited England, Scotland, and France for a month. I paid for the trip with money I'd saved since childhood.

So, I learned that time does make money grow. If you have a clear picture of your goal, one that you know will be worth it, you can wait for your money to grow bigger.

When you deduct 10% from your salary every month for savings, you don't see it or touch it. You don't even have to account for it—you just do it and live on the 90% that's left.

COLLECT COINS IN A JAR

You've heard the saying "A penny saved is a penny earned"? The Japanese might say, "A penny saved could save your life."

Take a look around and you'll find pennies, nickels, dimes and quarters here and there inside your home—in drawers, on  shelves, in pockets, and so forth. Look in the car, too.

At the end of each day, your pockets, wallet, or purse may be heavy with coins.

If you collect your coins every day, and put them in a jar, your collection will grow, and you won't even miss that money.

I usually count up about $85 in my jar after a period of six months.

This really helps, especially if you find yourself short on cash one day or if you are saving up for something special for yourself.

LUCKY MONEY (OTOSHIDAMA)

On New Year's Day, Japanese adults customarily give money to children.

This is called *otoshidama*. In the Edo period, wealthy families and large stores gave out small bags of *mochi* (rice cakes) and money, believing it would bring happiness for the new year. It was handed out in small, brightly decorated envelopes, called *pochibukuro*, similar to Chinese red envelopes. This custom still continues to this day.

Usually, the money is given to children, from infants to young adults up to age twenty. The amount of money given depends on each family and the age of the child, although each child in a family usually receives the same so no one feels slighted.

The point of this custom is that even young kids have the opportunity to learn the value of money. They can touch it and count it and realize what it is they have.

Children from small to big can then develop an appreciation of money.

When a child has cash, a parent can help him or her recognize what it is worth. The child has the opportunity to think about whether to save it or spend it.

I think it is a good idea for young kids to receive money on days of celebration.

It symbolizes good luck and prosperity. Children think happy thoughts about it.

HOUSEHOLD BOOKKEEPING

In a bad domestic and global economy, is there anything that sells well?

When I was visiting Japan in the winter of 2008, I saw a news report broadcast from a bookstore. The reporter was saying that a current bestseller was the household expense journal.

When I heard this, I thought of my mother. During her whole life, she kept track of the household expenses in her own personal notebook.

When the Japanese economy was soaring, people did not care about keeping track of their expenditures.

But there's been a revival of conscientious spending and saving. People are trying to handle their money better and live within their incomes.

So, I visited a bookstore, and I found twenty to thirty different kinds of these expense journals.

I bought a very thin and simple one with plastic pockets for receipts.

You don't really need to buy an expense journal; you can use a regular notebook.

Make entries for income and all your expenses: gas and electricity, phones, insurance, water, credit card payments, food, and so forth. Don't forget savings.

When you are keeping track of your money, you probably spend less and save more.

MAKE A GRAPH OF MONTHLY EXPENSES

Keeping a record of what you spend is a good idea, but you really want to do more to improve your financial situation.

A graph gives you a clear picture of how you are handling

your money. You can compare the results every month to see if you are improving or not.

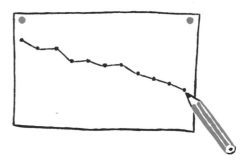

Try graphing what you spend for utilities, water, cell phone, long distance, and so forth.

If you think you are overpaying, you can contact customer service and get advice on better ways to save on your services.

Looking at the graph is fun, and challenges you to create a new plan.

A "TRUST" FUND

Is it really hard for you to save? Does your money just disappear?

Sometimes you need a little help from your friends.

I first heard about this savings plan in Japan, but I found out that some people in the USA use it, too. And it works for them.

I call it a trust fund, but you can call it a money pool or anything you like. Let's say you work in a relatively small office with about ten people, or there are ten of you in the same department at a larger company. You can learn "to trust." Each one of you will put $100 per week into the fund. At the end of each week, one of you gets $1,000. The point is, whether you are the first or tenth person to get the lump sum, you keep putting in your $100 share every week. It's that simple. It forces you to save. I think this is a good community-building exercise. It's an opportunity to create strength and harmony within your group. Everybody wins. But, you can imagine that trust might go bust! Choose the members of your team carefully. Establish written rules and agreements, signed by all.

STAY HEALTHY AFTER AGE SIXTY AND SAVE $215,000!

We know that health is more important than anything else.

The older we get, the more we realize how essential good health is. And yes, money can buy health.

Even if you don't have enough savings for retirement, your good health can save you as much as $215,000, according to Fidelity Investments. They figured that a couple currently in their mid-sixties who aren't covered by employer-sponsored insurance for retirees could spend about that much for out-of-pocket medical expenses by the time they're eighty-five years old.

So, I say, get healthy! Drink green tea every day, improve your diet, reduce stress, do easy exercise, and don't waste money or energy. Green tea living may be even more valuable to you than an insurance plan.

eco-resources

For more information, explore my website, where I provide important links to strategies for Green Tea Living.

Green Tea Living
www.greentealiving.com

The following are websites where you can buy green tea (if you can't get it from a local shop or want to try different types).

Zencha
www.zencha.net

ShizuokaTea
www.shizuokatea.com

Here are several websites to help you learn more about the topics in this book and obtain some of the items I've mentioned.

Green Tea Lovers
www.greentealovers.com/greenteausesrecipes.htm
Recipes using tea leaves and brewed tea.

Tea Navigator
www.teanavigator.com
All about tea, including tea wares, recipes, health information, and a brief list of tearooms.

Asian Food Grocer

www.asianfoodgrocer.com

An online source of tofu, miso, *natto*, *konnyaku*, and other healthy Japanese foods.

Daiso

www.daisojapan.com

A great variety of Japanese "livingware."

J-Box

www.jbox.com/CTTR

Lots of Japanese goods, including *bento* boxes and accessories.

Jun Japanese Gifts

www.jun-gifts.com/specialcollections/getasandals/getasandals.htm

Traditional geta sandals.

Furoshiki

www.furoshiki.com

Wrapping cloths, with diagrams and suggested uses.

Tozzok

www.tozzok.com

A source for five-toe socks.

About the Author

Toshimi A. Kayaki was born and raised in Japan. After college, she worked at an advertising company. Later she moved to Hollywood, where she wrote for a magazine and researched her first book. Upon returning to Japan, she published *There's No Job a Woman Can't Do*. She moved to the USA again in 1989. Toshimi has written for newspapers, magazines, and advertising agencies, and she has been a radio and TV reporter. She has published 22 books, most of them related to cultural comparisons, women's issues, housekeeping hints, and self-improvement. Toshimi lives in the San Francisco Bay Area with her husband, Sam, and son, Julian. She also has a son, Nicholas, who lives in Japan. Visit Toshimi's website at www.greentealiving.com.